Frederic Dan Huntington

Lessons for the Instruction of Children in the Christian life

Frederic Dan Huntington

Lessons for the Instruction of Children in the Christian life

ISBN/EAN: 9783744762649

Printed in Europe, USA, Canada, Australia, Japan

Cover: Foto ©Lupo / pixelio.de

More available books at **www.hansebooks.com**

Our Lord's Parables.

LESSONS

FOR THE

INSTRUCTION OF CHILDREN IN THE
CHRISTIAN LIFE.

BY THE
REV. F. D. HUNTINGTON, D. D.,
RECTOR OF EMMANUEL CHURCH, BOSTON.

BOSTON:
E. P. DUTTON AND COMPANY,
135 WASHINGTON STREET.
1868.

CONTENTS.

LESSON		PAGE
I.	On Parables, as used in the Teachings of Jesus Christ	1
II.	On the Books in which the Parables of the Saviour are recorded	5
III.	Parable of the Diseased and Single Eye	10
IV.	Parable of the Birds and the Lilies of the Field	15
V.	Parable of the Sower	21
VI.	Parable of the Tares	27
VII.	Parable of the Mustard-seed	32
VIII.	Parable of the Leaven	36
IX.	Parables of the Treasure in a Field, and of the Pearl of Great Price	40
X.	Parable of the Net	45
XI.	Parable of the Growing Grain	49
XII.	Parable of the Bread	53
XIII.	Parable of the Unforgiving Servant	56
XIV.	Parable of the Laborers in the Vineyard	61
XV.	Parable of the Good Samaritan	65
XVI.	Parable of the Man at Rest at Night	70
XVII.	Parable of the Man with many Goods	75
XVIII.	Parable of the Master and his Servants	79
XIX.	Parable of the Barren Fig-tree	83
XX.	Parable of the Great Supper	86
XXI.	Parables of the Tower, and of the King going to War	92
XXII.	Parable of the Lost Sheep, and of the Lost Piece of Silver	96
XXIII.	Parable of the Prodigal Son	101
XXIV.	Parable of the Unjust Steward	107
XXV.	Parable of the Rich Man and Lazarus	114
XXVI.	Parable of the Man and his Servant	118

CONTENTS.

LESSON		PAGE
XXVII.	Parable of the Unjust Judge	122
XXVIII.	Parable of the Publican and the Pharisee	128
XXIX.	Parable of the Ten Pounds	132
XXX.	Parable of the Two Sons	136
XXXI.	Parable of the Vineyard let out to Husbandmen	140
XXXII.	Parable of the Marriage-Feast	144
XXXIII.	Parable of the Ten Virgins	148
XXXIV.	Parable of the Talents	152
XXXV.	Parable of the Sheep and the Goats	156

NOTE.

It is the belief of the writer, that a wrong is done to children when they are treated as incapable of grasping the great points of spiritual doctrine revealed in the New Testament, and as if *to be Christians* were something that they must wait for, as an attainment of later years. The main object, therefore, has been to apply the practical doctrines of Christ, illustrated as they are with peculiar power in His Parables, — Repentance, Faith, Purity, Fidelity, Self-control, Truthfulness, Justice, Mercy, Devotion, Love, — with all possible simplicity, to the hearts of the young. Subordinate to this, the purpose has been twofold : first, to transfer the learner into the scenes and customs amidst which these Parables were actually spoken by the Saviour; and secondly, to bring the sacred influence of the Parables into the familiar sphere where the scholars are daily living. On the one hand, it has been thus sought to throw light on the original force and meaning of these beautiful passages ; and on the other, to secure a direct application of them to present duties.

DIRECTIONS.

WHEN an answer is long, and consists in the enumeration of several particulars, it may be given in parts by two or more scholars. So, also, in reciting or reading the parable that constitutes the lesson.

Some important questions are repeated in different parts of the volume, and the teacher will find it well to repeat many others, in the way of a review.

When a paraphrase, or explanation of an expression, is given, the Scriptural expression itself should always be repeated in connection with it.

Some of the Lessons will probably be found too long for a single exercise. It has been thought best, however, not to break the unity by a formal division, but rather to leave the teacher to separate the examination of each parable according to his own judgment.

It is very far from being desired that either the teacher or the pupil should adopt, in the class, precisely the language that is set down in these pages. Clauses are frequently thrown into the interrogatories that are intended entirely as suggestions to the teacher. Every intelligent teacher will no doubt find some things to be omitted, and many things to be enlarged upon. And the most faithful will not be satisfied that the scholars should literally repeat what is here written, but will encourage them to use these forms of expression as helps, while they frame their own replies.

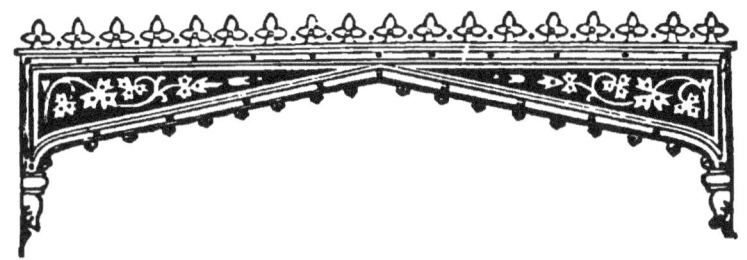

LESSONS ON THE PARABLES.

LESSON I.

ON PARABLES, AS USED IN THE TEACHINGS OF JESUS CHRIST.

Q. What is a Parable?

A. It is a story told for the purpose of teaching some truth.

Q. Are the things that are related in parables things that have really happened just as they are told there?

A. They are not; the speaker or writer only *imagines* them to have happened.

Q. Are the persons who are spoken of in parables *real* persons?

A. Generally they are not; they exist only in the imagination or the thoughts, and therefore may be called imaginary persons.

Q. Is there any falsehood in thus relating things that never took place, and the actions of persons that never lived?

A. There is not, because it is always well understood by those that hear or read the parable that it was not intended to represent *facts*, but was meant as a fiction.

Q. What would make a parable a falsehood?

A. If the speaker or writer had any intention to deceive others, and to make them believe something that is not true, then he would be guilty of a falsehood.

Q. What, then, may a parable be said to be?

A. An indirect way of teaching truth by a fiction.

Q. What other name may be given to a parable?

A. It may be called an allegory; and sometimes it is only a comparison of one thing with another, for the sake of illustrating it, or making its meaning more plain.

Q. Suppose you wished to show some one how much better it is to be kind than to be selfish, how might you attempt to do it?

A. I might simply say that it is better to be kind than to be selfish.

Q. But would this be sure to make an impression, and be remembered?

A. It would not.

Q. How, then, might you make this important truth more striking and impressive?

A. I might use my imagination, and tell a story of two children, one of whom should be kind and the other selfish; I might give them names, and speak of them just as if they were real children; I might fancy a place for them to live in, and describe that; and then I might go on to show how much more noble, useful, and happy the kind child would be than the selfish one. This would be a parable; and I should show by it how much better kindness is than selfishness.

Q. Is it always mentioned, at the beginning or the end of a parable, what moral lesson it is designed to teach?

A. It is not; very often the occasion when it is spoken, or some circumstances about it, will help the hearer to make out very clearly what the right application of it is.

LESSONS ON THE PARABLES. 3

Q. Is this way of teaching much used now?

A. It is not, though among some nations it is more common than among us.

Q. What nations have been particularly fond of this mode of speaking?

A. The nations of eastern countries, and especially those of that part of Asia where the Jews lived, and where the Bible was mostly written.

Q. When a piece of writing contains a great many comparisons, figures, and images, what do you call it?

A. Poetical, because poetry abounds in such figures and comparisons; or imaginative, because the imagination of the writer is so lively in drawing these comparisons, and pointing out the resemblance between one thing and another.

Q. What, now, was the reason that those people, among whom the Bible was written, were so much in the habit of using parables, and other figures of speech?

A. They had, naturally, very poetical and imaginative minds.

Q. What are some of the parables of the Old Testament?

A. There is one recorded in 2 Sam. xii., which was spoken by Nathan; another is in 2 Sam. xiv.

Q. Whom were these New Testament parables spoken by?

A. By the Saviour, who included them in His discourses, with precepts, and other instructions.

Q. What was His object in delivering so many parables?

A. To make His followers feel the importance of their various duties to God and to their fellow-men.

Q. As we read these parables even now, more than

eighteen hundred years after they were first delivered, how do they still seem to us?

A. Very beautiful and very interesting.

Q. How does Jesus make spiritual realities and duties simple and easy to our understanding?

A. He compares them, in these parables, to common objects, — objects that we are familiar with, and can see or hear or taste or touch.

Q. What shall we find, as we go on, to be some of the natural objects that are compared by Christ to spiritual things?

A. Grain, sheep, a candle, a pearl. He compares goodness to mustard-seed; a sinful man to a tree with bad fruit, and to thorns and thistles; and good men to trees with good fruit.

Q. What is one peculiarity of the parables of the Saviour?

A. These stories are remarkably natural in themselves; that is, they relate things which are likely to happen, and have nothing strange or marvelous in them.

Q. What is another peculiarity about them?

A. Generally each parable relates to something that took place at the time when it was spoken, and sometimes to some object that was in sight at the moment. Luke xi. 1-9; xii. 16; xiv. 7; and perhaps Matt. xiii. 3-8.

Q. How do these parables of the Saviour illustrate His benevolence?

A. He longed to make his followers and all mankind feel the Truth that He came into the world to declare, because He knew that it would make them pure and holy and happy forever; and He spoke it in parables, because He knew that in that simple and engaging form it would be most likely to reach their hearts.

Q. What should you always seek first, when you read or study a parable?

A. To find out exactly what duty, or what religious lesson, Jesus intended to teach by that parable.

Q. What should you next endeavor to do?

A. To apply this lesson, whatever it is, to my own heart and my own conduct, so as to be made better by it.

Q. If you do this sincerely and earnestly, what may you always hope for as your reward?

A. I shall find my reward in the improvement of my own character, in the delightful feeling that I have done right, and in being sure that I have pleased my Heavenly Father. It will be as if I had been sitting at my Saviour's feet, and listening to him.

LESSON II.

ON THE BOOKS IN WHICH THE PARABLES OF THE SAVIOUR ARE RECORDED.

Q. If you had been among those first disciples of the Saviour who heard His gracious words and witnessed His holy example, what desire should you naturally have felt after He was put to death by His enemies, and had ascended from the world?

A. A desire to have some account of His wonderful teachings and actions written down and preserved.

Q. Does this desire seem to have been felt by those who were actually the companions and disciples of Christ in His earthly life?

A. It does; for we find that four of them did write

such accounts of their Master's life, and their four books have been placed one after another in the Bible.

Q. Who were these four disciples of Christ?

A. St. Matthew, St. Mark, St. Luke, and St. John.

Q. Where do you find the names of the twelve men that Jesus chose to be His disciples?

A. In St. Matthew x. and St. Luke vi.

Q. What is the meaning of the word "disciples"?

A. It means *learners*, and it is applied to these twelve because they were peculiarly called to be faithful learners of Christ their Master.

Q. What other name is given by Jesus, in these passages, to the "twelve"?

A. He calls them "apostles."

Q. Why does he call them "apostles"?

A. The word *apostle* signifies a *messenger*, or a *person sent forth;* and it was given by Jesus to these twelve because he sent them forth to teach His Gospel to mankind, and plant His Church.

Q. Which of the four disciples, mentioned above as having written histories or biographies of Jesus, belonged to the company of these Twelve Apostles?

A. St. Matthew and St. John.

Q. What name is often given to these four books?

A. They are named the *Four Gospels*.

Q. Why are they named so?

A. Because each one of them contains a *gospel;* that is, a record of that divine revelation of religious truth which God made to the world through the life and words and sacrifice of Jesus Christ.

Q. What does the writer of each of them do?

A. He gives a faithful narrative of what was said and done by the Saviour during His ministry in Judea.

LESSONS ON THE PARABLES. 7

Q. How are these four Gospels commonly designated?

A. By the names of the writers; as, the *Gospel by St. Matthew*, or *according to St. Matthew*, or St. Mark, or St. Luke, or St. John.

Q. In what other sense is the word *gospel* used?

A. It is often used without any reference to these particular writings, and to signify, in general, that whole revelation of spiritual truth, and of God's fatherly love and mercy, which came through Christ. See Acts xx. 24; Eph. i. 13.

Q. What is the difference between these two meanings?

A. In the latter case, the *doctrine* or *message* itself is intended; in the other, the *written account* of that message, the *record* of that doctrine, is intended.

Q. What are the writers of these four Gospels called?

A. Evangelists.

Q. Why are they called so?

A. From the word *evangel*, which means *gospel*.

Q. What is the original meaning of *evangel*, or of the word in the Greek language from which it is derived?

A. A message of *good news*, or *glad tidings*.

Q. Why is this an appropriate name for the gospel?

A. It is *glad tidings* because it shows us how to escape from sin and misery, how to be holy and happy; and it promises forgiveness from our Father in heaven when we repent, believe, and are baptized.

Q. What language were these books written in?

A. In the Greek.

Q. When and where were they all translated into English, as we now have them?

A. More than two hundred years ago, in the time of King James the First, in England.

Q. For what reasons are we to regard these books as accurate and trustworthy?

A. They were written by honest and good men, inspired by the Holy Ghost, who kept them clear from error; they were written within a few years after Christ was put to death, and while the events they describe were fresh in their memory; and they were received as correct by the men of their own time, who were acquainted with all the circumstances.

Q. What worthy tribute has been paid to these accounts by all generations since they were written?

A. While other records have perished or been set aside, these have been preserved, reverenced, and studied with delight, by Christian persons in all ages.

Q. Ought we not to be especially thankful that we have more than one such account?

A. We ought; for what was omitted by one or more of these writers, we find mentioned by another: and every thing that Jesus did or said is unspeakably valuable to us all.

Q. What excellent means had they for knowing the *truth* concerning the matters that they described?

A. St. Matthew and St. John were companions of the Saviour, seeing what He did and hearing what He said; while St. Mark and St. Luke were intimately acquainted with those who were His companions and disciples: so that in either case their information was direct and exact.

Q. Do these writers thrust into their books their own opinions or comments or guesses, or any commendation of their Master?

A. They do not; but with a dignified simplicity which makes us believe they were sincere and true, they show us the Son of God, and give us His own words and deeds.

Q. Did these writers always put down the events just in the order in which they happened?

A. They did not; but that order has been pretty clearly made out by scholars who have compared their accounts together. St. Luke follows the order of events.

Q. Where are you told who St. Matthew (or " Levi," his other name) was, and how he was led to attach himself to Jesus?

A. In his own Gospel, ix. 9; and in other places he is mentioned among the other Apostles.

Q. Who was St. Mark, the author of the second Gospel?

A. St. Mark, or " John Mark," or " Marcus," as his name is sometimes written, was the son of a pious woman living at Jerusalem, — a companion and friend of Peter, Paul, and Barnabas, disciples of our Lord. See Acts xii. 12, 25; xiii. 5, 13; 1 Pet. v. 13; 2 Tim. iv. 11; Col. iv. 10.

Q. Who was St. Luke, the author of the third Gospel?

A. He seems to have been a fellow-traveller with St. Paul, a friend of other disciples, a physician, and a devout Christian. He wrote also the Acts of the Apostles. See Col. iv. 14; 2 Tim. iv. 11. Compare Acts i. 1, and his Gospel, i. 3.

Q. Who was St. John, the author of the fourth Gospel?

A. The " beloved disciple " of Jesus, the son of Zebedee, a fisherman on the Lake of Galilee, and probably near to the Saviour during His ministry. See Matt. iv. 21; Mark i. 19, 20; John xiii. 23; xxi. 20–25; Acts iii. 1.

Q. Where are these four Evangelists supposed to have written their Gospels?

A. St. Matthew in Judea; St. Mark at Rome; St. Luke in Greece; and St. John at Ephesus, in Asia Minor.

Q. Shall we find all the parables of the Saviour recorded by each one of these Evangelists?

A. We shall not; for these, like His other instructions, are written in part by one and in part by another; but from the four we may collect them all, and arrange them in order.

LESSON III.

PARABLE OF THE DISEASED AND SINGLE EYE.

Q. Where is the parable of the diseased and single eye recorded?

A. In the Gospel of St. Matthew, chap. vi., verses 22 and 23.

Q. Will you repeat those verses?

Q. Does either of the other Evangelists relate to us these words of the Saviour?

A. St. Luke relates them in chap. xi., from verse 33 to verse 36, of his Gospel, with a few verbal differences.

Q. What do you mean by "Evangelists"?

A. (See one of the answers in the preceding Lesson.)

Q. What do you mean by "verbal differences"?

A. That some of the words used by St. Luke, in his account of this parable, are different from the words used by St. Matthew, while the sense, or meaning, is substantially the same.

LESSONS ON THE PARABLES.

Q. In the midst of what discourse did Christ utter this parable?

A. In His Sermon on the Mount.

Q. What is the Sermon on the Mount?

A. It is that address, or sermon, spoken by Christ to his followers, in which He sets forth some of the great principles and most important truths which He came into the world to teach.

Q. Why is it called the Sermon *on the Mount*?

A. Because Christ stood on a mount, or elevation of land, when He delivered it to the multitudes, who were on the side of the hill.

Q. Where is this mountain?

A. It is near Capernaum in Galilee.

Q. What and where is Capernaum?

A. It is a city, near the northern extremity of the Sea of Galilee. (See Map of Palestine.)

Q. Will you point out, on the map, the direction of this city from Nazareth, where Jesus had been brought up? (See St. Matt. ii. 23, and iii. 13.)

Q. Will you point out nearly the place where Jesus delivered the Sermon on the Mount, and its direction from Bethlehem, where He was born? (St. Matt. ii. 1.)

Q. How do we know that Jesus was in this place at this time?

A. By turning to St. Matthew, chap. v., verse 1, where the Sermon on the Mount commences, and comparing that verse with St. Matthew iii., verses 13, 18, and 23.

Q. Looking now at the parable itself,—what does the Saviour mean when He says, "The light of the body is the eye"?

A. He means that it is through our eyes that light

enters the body; that it is only by means of the eye that we discern the light and see all outward objects; while without the eye we should be in darkness and see nothing. The eye is to the body what a candle is to a room in the night.

Q. How do you understand the phrase, "If thine eye be *single*"?

A. It means, "If thine eye be *clear, pure, in a healthy state*, so as to perceive objects distinctly, without any blur or dimness."

Q. With such eyes, what will be the result?

A. "The whole body shall be full of light"; that is, light will be transmitted *clearly;* the vision will be perfect.

Q. What is meant by the next expression,—"If thine eye be evil"?

A. "If thine eye is *diseased,* or *blinded.*"

Q. If the eye is in this state, what will be the consequence?

A. All will be dark; nothing can be seen,—neither the light of sun, nor moon, nor stars, nor any thing around us.

Q. Will you now read St. Luke's account of the same passage in our Lord's instructions?

A. (See St. Luke xi. 33, and three verses following.)

Q. What is taught in verse 33 of this chapter in St. Luke, which is not found in connection with this parable in St. Matthew, but which is found in Matt. v. 15?

A. That we ought not to cover up the light of knowledge and goodness; for that would be like hiding a candle under any close vessel, as a bushel; but that we should act so that the truth may shine forth in our good example, as the beams of a candle on a candlestick shine far around it.

Q. Will you state what Jesus intended to teach by this parable?

A. He intended to convey by it a *spiritual truth*, and not merely to say, that unless the bodily eye is in a sound condition we cannot see.

Q. What is that spiritual truth?

A. He teaches us that our minds must be kept pure.

Q. Why must they be kept pure?

A. Because if they are not, they cannot receive the light of His truth any more than a diseased eye can receive the light of the sun.

Q. What must we strive to keep our minds pure from?

A. From all sinful thoughts, and wrong desires, and base passions.

Q. What are some of the things that corrupt the mind?

A. Selfishness corrupts it; so does intemperance; so does the love of money; so do anger, impurity, envy, and falsehood.

Q. What effect do these things have on our spiritual natures, — our souls?

A. They hinder our souls from growing in wisdom, benevolence, justice, charity, or in any Christian virtue.

Q. How can they be said to make our souls "blind"?

A. They so engross our thoughts with earthly things that we are *blind* to duty and excellence, and *do not see* the beauty of being good, nor the happiness of loving and serving Christ.

Q. What particular sin had Jesus in His view, probably, when He spoke this parable?

A. Worldly-mindedness, or loving the pleasures, and luxuries, and comforts of this life more than our Father in heaven.

Q. What reason is there for supposing that Christ alluded particularly to this sin?

A. In the preceding passage He had just been speaking of the importance of having our treasures laid up in heaven, and not on the earth. (See verses 19, 20, and 21.)

Q. What does this mean?

A. That we should prize things that cannot perish, such as goodness, kindness, purity, meekness, truth, as far more precious than silver or gold, houses or lands, amusements or dress, food or drink.

Q. How does a worldly spirit blind our souls?

A. It makes us satisfied with our present pleasures, and turns off our thoughts and affections from nobler subjects.

Q. What will become of those pleasures that are earthly, and that depend on our bodies?

A. They will vanish when our bodies die.

Q. How will it be with that spiritual happiness that comes from doing right?

A. That is much grander and deeper in itself, and it will remain with us forever in heaven.

Q. Should we not be as anxious to have our spiritual discernment good, as our bodily eyesight?

A. We should; because the things that we see with our souls are greater and better than the things that we see with our eyes.

Q. How then may we keep the vision of our souls "single," or "clear," so that we may understand the truth?

A. By shunning vice and sin; by obeying our consciences; by being just; by speaking the truth; by being generous; by praying to God.

Q. What great motive have we for keeping our hearts so pure?

A. The purer and better our hearts are, the more of Christ's truth shall we understand, the more like Christ shall we be, and the more will our Heavenly Father love us.

Q. What other passage in the Sermon on the Mount does this parable remind you of?

A. Verses 3, 4, and 5 of chap. vii.

Q. Will you read them and explain them?

A. The eye is there compared to the soul; and Jesus teaches that we are very apt to discover and talk about other persons' faults, but forget our own; just as those who have great defects or "beams" in their own eyes are ready to reproach those who have only "motes" or little splinters in theirs.

―――◆―――

LESSON IV.

PARABLE OF THE BIRDS AND THE LILIES OF THE FIELD.

Q. WHERE do you find the passage containing the parable of the birds and the lilies?

A. In the Gospel of St. Matthew, chap. vi., from verse 26 to the close; and in the Gospel by St. Luke, chap. xii., from verse 22 to verse 30.

Q. Of what discourse does it form a part?

A. It is a part of Christ's Sermon on the Mount.

Q. Will you repeat this parable, as it is in St. Matthew?

Q. What is Jesus teaching us here?

A. That we ought to be more anxious to be good, than to be well dressed, or to have delicate food.

Q. In order to see how Christ introduces this passage, and to find the course of thought that led Him to it, will you look back, and read verses 24 and 25?

Q. What is the *Mammon* spoken of in verse 24?

A. Riches, or worldly gain.

Q. If one should love money more than his Maker, what might be said of him?

A. That money, or wealth, is his god, and that he worships a money-god, or Mammon.

Q. Is not a person who loves pleasure more than duty an idolater?

A. In one sense he is so, as much as if he offered his worship to a carved image of wood or stone, or to the sun or stars; for he is devoted to earthly things more than to God.

Q. What is one way in which young persons show this bad spirit?

A. If they would rather do wrong than to give up a social party, or resign some favorite plan of pleasure, then they love Mammon more than God.

Q. What is meant when it is said, "Ye cannot serve God and Mammon"?

A. That we cannot love both God and earthly things equally; that we must either love God more than worldly convenience and pleasure, and thus be good, or we shall certainly love worldly things more than God, and thus be wicked.

Q. Is there any such thing possible as your being neither good nor wicked?

A. There is not; I must be either the one or the other.

Q. Where are you told which of these you ought to be?

A. I am told by my own conscience, as well as in the Bible.

Q. Does not Jesus tell you which you ought to be, in this very passage?

A. He does, in verse 25.

Q. What do you understand by that verse?

A. That when I am thinking of what is really important in my life, I should esteem what I eat, and drink, and wear, and all my outward possessions, as of much less value than my religious character.

Q. Why is this?

A. Because "meat," or food, and "raiment," or clothing, belong wholly to my body, which is to die and decay; but goodness and truth belong to my spiritual part, my soul, which is to live forever.

Q. When it is said, "Take no thought," &c., is it intended that we should not provide *any* support for our bodies and for our friends?

A. It is not, for the Bible teaches us that we ought to labor and earn our living industriously.

Q. Will you mention some passages where this is said?

A. Eph. iv. 28; Rom. xii. 11; 1 Tim. v. 8; Exod. xx. 9.

Q. How are you to make this labor innocent, and guard against becoming excessively attached to your gains?

A. By always working in a religious spirit, and always preferring what is right to any selfish enjoyment.

Q. Will you read verse 26, and tell what you understand by it?

A. That if God keeps the birds of the air alive, and provides for them while they do not lay up stores for themselves, we may be sure He will take care of us, who have foresight and reason, and hands to work with.

Q. What is meant by the expression, "Are ye not much *better* than they"?

A. Christ means that every human being must be of more worth in the sight of God than a bird can be.

Q. Why is this so?

A. Because every man, woman, and child has an immortal soul, a conscience, reason, powers of thought, and speech.

Q. How is the dignity of a human being set forth in the Bible?

A. He is represented as being made "in the image of God"; as being "but little lower than the angels"; as the chief of all God's creatures on the earth.

Q. If God has exalted us so highly in our nature, what ought we to do?

A. We ought to live worthily of such a privilege, and to remember what a terrible thing it is to pollute such a nature with any sin.

Q. How do you suppose Jesus came to compare men with the birds, in this place?

A. It is very probable, that, as He was delivering this discourse on a mountain, in the open air, He saw birds flying near Him, and pointed to them as He spoke.

Q. What would He teach us by this comparison?

A. That we should feel our dependence on God for every thing, and not be over anxious about the future events of life.

Q. How does He continue this sentiment in verse 27?

A. He reminds us that we cannot increase our own stature, or prolong our own life, in the least; that it is God alone who makes us live and grow; and that, do what we will, we have not power to make ourselves one cubit taller, or one moment younger, than we are.

Q. How much is a cubit?

A. It was a measure used by the Jews, in the time of Christ, of about one foot and a half in length.

Q. Many persons show a great deal of attention and care about dress; what does Jesus say to them, in verse 28?

A. That they should learn, from the fact that God makes the lilies so beautiful, that it is really His power and love, and not their own wisdom, that supplies them with clothing.

Q. Is it not likely that this mention of lilies was suggested to Jesus as He was speaking, as that of the birds was?

A. It is; and that He saw, where He stood, an abundance of these splendid flowers, which are very beautiful in that country, covering the fields around Him.

Q. Why does He say that Solomon, in his magnificent robes, was not arrayed, or dressed so richly, as a simple lily?

A. To show that the utmost skill of man is inferior to the wonderful workmanship of God, who creates and colors the flowers.

Q. Why does He select Solomon in particular?

A. Because Solomon was once the king of this same

Jewish people, and was distinguished for his riches, living in a brilliant palace of gold, and ivory, and precious wood.

Q. Where can you find an account of Solomon and his great wealth?

A. In 2 Chronicles, chap. ix.

Q. How ought it to affect us to see, that, after all his pains and expenditures, a man is far less glorious in his outward appearance than a simple and pure lily?

A. It should teach us to regard our outward appearance as of far less moment than good dispositions within the heart.

Q. What else should it teach us?

A. What is said in verse 30, — that if God takes such excellent care of even the little flowers and the grass, as well as of great worlds and nations, He will also remember us, whom He loves as His children.

Q. Will you explain the expression, "Which to-day is, and to-morrow is cast into the oven"?

A. Jesus represents this flowering grass as being so frail, that while it stands green and flourishing one day, the next day it may be cut down for fuel to heat ovens.

Q. If what is so frail is adorned and beautified by God, what should we feel respecting our own lot in life?

A. That every thing which we really need will be given us from above.

Q. From this whole passage, what is the chief lesson you should learn?

A. To trust entirely in the goodness of God, my Heavenly Father.

Q. When you find yourself feeling anxious about the future, what should you call to mind?

A. The words in verse 34, bidding me let every day bring its own cares, and not to borrow trouble in advance.

Q. When you find any of your worldly plans perplexing you, what precept should you remember?

A. That one in verse 33, where I am told that I must seek first after righteousness, and to do the will of God, as more important than any thing else can possibly be.

Q. When you are disposed to be vain of your personal appearance, what should extinguish your pride?

A. The thought, that after all I am less beautiful than many things out in the fields of nature; and therefore I should be humble and modest.

Q. Seeing that you are allowed by Jesus to put your trust and confidence in your Heavenly Father, and know that He is your friend, what should you do in return?

A. I should daily thank Him, with all my heart, that He does take such kind care of me and of all my friends; and I should labor and pray, both to do what He commands me, and to bear, patiently and cheerfully, whatever He sends upon me.

LESSON V.

PARABLE OF THE SOWER.

Q. Where do you find the parable of the sower?

A. It is written by St. Matthew in chap. xiii. of his Gospel; by Mark in chap. iv.; and by St. Luke in chap. viii.

Q. What is the reason the accounts given by these

three Evangelists are not precisely alike in their language?

A. Each one of them used such words as occurred to his own mind, under the direction of the Spirit, without copying the others.

Q. What reason have you to believe that all of them have given us the parable *substantially* the same as it was delivered by Jesus Himself?

A. The fact, that, while their words are not exactly alike, they all convey the same *sense*, the same *meaning*.

Q. Suppose the three had recorded the parable in precisely the same words, what might you possibly conclude?

A. That two of them copied their accounts from the third, or else that they all copied them from some other person; but now we have the independent testimony of three different writers to show us that Jesus did actually speak this parable.

Q. Where was Jesus at this time?

A. He was by the shore of the Sea of Galilee (Matt. xiii. 1), not far from Capernaum. (See map.)

Q. Turning to the account as it is given by St. Luke, chap. viii., will you read the parable itself, in verses 5–8. What can you suppose might have suggested this parable to the thoughts of the Saviour?

A. He might have seen near Him the fields where sowers sowed their seed, and perhaps a sower at work.

Q. He imagines a sower to scatter some of his seed by the wayside: how would this be likely to happen?

A. In that country the farms belonging to different men were divided from each other by paths or roads, so that the highways passed close by the edge of the ploughed land, and the sower would be very apt to scatter some of his grain into them.

Q. Why would the birds of the air find the grain there, " by the wayside," more than in the field itself?

A. Because the ground was trodden hard in the path; but in the field the soil was light and soft, and the seed was soon covered by it. Flocks of birds are often seen in the East hovering about the sowers.

Q. The reason why this part of the seed sown did not produce any fruit, then, was because it was eaten up by the birds as soon as it was scattered : what other portion of the seed failed to produce fruit, and why?

A. That which happened to drop on rocks and stones could not take root, of course, and was soon dried up and spoiled by the sun (verse 6).

Q. What was the difficulty with another part of the seed?

A. It fell where it had no chance to grow, because the ground was already covered and shaded by thorns or weeds which strangled it.

Q. What part was really fruitful (verse 8)?

A. That which was scattered on the moist and fertile earth which had been ploughed and prepared for it.

Q. What does Jesus mean by the latter part of verse 8?

A. He means, as in other places where He uses the same expression, to call particular attention to what He is saying.

Q. When His disciples ask him (verse 9) to explain this parable, what do you understand Him to say in reply (verse 10)?

A. He says: "You, my disciples, may understand the deep truths and doctrines that I teach" (that is, "the mysteries of the kingdom of God"); "but I am obliged to teach others, less acquainted with me than you are, conceited and proud of their knowledge, by putting my instructions into these simple parables; for though they see all my wonderful works, yet they have no faith in me, and though they hear my precepts, they do not obey them. By speaking to them in parables, or plain stories and comparisons, I shall prove them whether they are teachable and simple-hearted."

Q. Will you now read the five following verses, which contain Christ's own explanation of the meaning of this parable? What, then, does Christ signify by the "seed" spoken of in this parable?

A. The instructions of His gospel, — those spiritual truths which He gives us to make our lives pure and good.

Q. What is the "field," or soil, in which these instructions are sown?

A. The human heart, — all our hearts.

Q. Jesus speaks of four kinds of persons, who hear His truth with very different results; will you describe the first of these, mentioned in verse 12?

A. Those belong to this class, who, after they have heard religious instruction, take no pains to remember what they have heard, but let other things take away the good impression from their minds, as the birds caught up the grain that lay on the surface of the road. And this is because evil thoughts have run through their hearts so long and so often as to trample them down and make them hard as a road.

Q. What is true of such characters?

A. They are superficial, empty, and trifling; for they forget what they hear, and worldly vanities drive away their serious thoughts.

Q. What are you to understand by the phrase " the devil taketh away the word "?

A. That the Tempter, through our own bad desires, or bad companions, prevents our keeping the right way.

Q. What is our duty, then, if we wish to " believe and be saved "?

A. To remember all good instructions that we receive from the Bible, from the Church, from our teachers or parents; and then to act upon them, carrying them out in our life.

Q. What if you find it hard to do this?

A. Then I must strive the more earnestly, resist the temptation, and pray to God to help me.

Q. In what case would you belong to this class of characters?

A. If I were to neglect, through the week, the lessons I learn on the Sabbath, instead of practising them in all that I do.

Q. Who are the persons that are compared in this parable to the " rock " on which some of the seed fell (verse 13)?

A. They are those who go a little farther in the right way than the class before mentioned; they believe the truth they hear, and begin to practice the good; but when they are thrown into strong temptations they allow their virtue to be overcome, and fall back into sin.

Q. Why is religious truth on their heart like seed on the rock?

A. Because it may begin to germinate, or take root, but it is soon dried up and perishes. The warmth of the rock, heated by the sun, made the seed start " forthwith."

Q. What are some of the things which often break up our religious characters and separate us from Christ?

A. Our selfishness; our evil passions, like anger and revenge; thoughtlessness in gay society; pride in having our own way; our desire to gratify some wrong appetite. These scorch the seed.

Q. How ought we to manage these?

A. We ought to control them all by our Christian principles.

Q. How can we strengthen ourselves in these Christian principles?

A. By studying the example and precepts of Christ, and praying for the help of God's Holy Spirit.

Q. Need we, then, be afraid to join our companions and share their amusements?

A. We need not, for we shall then be safe against temptation.

Q. Who are they whose hearts are like the soil choked with "thorns"?

A. They are the persons that allow themselves to love money, pleasure, or their earthly business, more than they love duty and God (verse 14).

Q. If this is their case, will they not be liable to commit sin continually?

A. They will; for though their consciences and the Bible both warn them not to do wrong, they will not heed the warning.

Q. Must not this be an awful condition for any soul to be in?

A. It must make us miserable, and destroy all the peace and glory of the soul. It chokes our true life.

Q. Would it not be very ungrateful?

A. It would; for we must remember how much our Heavenly Father and our Saviour have kindly done to lead us in a better course.

Q. When our inclination points one way, and duty another, which shall we obey?

A. Follow Christ, who "pleased not himself."

Q. If we do this, what shall we be like?

A. Like that "good ground," in which the seeds of truth and goodness take root and grow up into a plant and bear fruit.

Q. What will our hearts be then?

A. "Honest and good hearts," full of joy, nobleness, and the peace that Christ gives.

Q. If we continue so, choosing duty rather than sin and shame, what will be the spiritual fruit that our lives will bring forth?

A. Righteous actions and pure affections; our conversation will be kind and true; we shall be gentle, and upright, and devout.

Q. What, then, shall be your resolution?

A. That whatever I learn from Christ, I will keep and obey.

Q. What is God's blessing on every faithful act and feeling?

A. It enriches the heart and prepares it for yet greater readiness and fruitfulness afterwards.

LESSON VI.

PARABLE OF THE TARES.

Q. Where do you find the parable of the tares?

A. In St. Matthew's Gospel, xiii. 24–30.

Q. It is said, verse 24, that Jesus put forth *another* parable; what parable had he just spoken?

A. The parable of the sower, in the last lesson.

Q. What makes it appear natural that the one should have suggested and led to the other?

A. They both relate to the sowing of seed in the field.

Q. What is that "kingdom of heaven" which Jesus compares here to the man sowing seed?

A. That phrase has different shades of meaning; but it seems here to mean God's plan of planting the truth of the gospel in the minds of men, which is His Church.

Q. What is that *truth* represented by in this parable?

A. By the *good seed* which was sown.

Q. What is represented by the "tares" which some enemy came in the night, just after the good seed was sown. and sowed on the same field (verse 25)?

A. Those bad influences which sometimes come upon our hearts after we have been receiving Christian instruction, — such as the example of wicked persons, or some temptation to do wrong.

Q. In the parable, Christ imagines the wheat which sprung from the good seed, and the tares which sprung from the bad seed that the enemy sowed, to be growing together; why would not this be perceived as soon as they began to grow (verse 26)?

A. We are told that the stalks or *blades* of the good and bad plants were very much alike in their appearance.

Q. When the servants, or workmen, of this householder, or owner of the land, saw that the tares and wheat were both growing, what did they do?

A. See verse 27.

Q. What does the owner of the land reply to them?

A. He knows that he sowed only the seed of good wheat, and therefore he tells them some enemy must have come secretly and scattered the seed of tares on his field.

Q. What in fact, are these *tares* ?

A. They are weeds, called "darnel," which grow in that country (Judea) where Jesus was speaking; though they resemble the wheat in appearance, they are poisonous, and injure the grain.

Q. What do the servants offer to do ?

A. To go and pull up these tares at once (verse 28).

Q. What reason does the owner of the field give for not allowing them to do so?

A. He fears that, while they pull up the tares, the roots of the tares will also bring up out of the ground the wheat standing with them (verse 29).

Q. What course does he command ?

A. See verse 30.

Q. Where does Jesus give an explanation of the meaning of this parable ?

A. In verses 37–43.

Q. Whom does the householder, or owner of the land, represent ?

A. "The Son of Man," Jesus Christ our Saviour.

Q. What is the peculiar signification of this title?

A. Jesus, a perfect man, with human body, soul, and spirit, applies it to himself in great humility, to show that He has feelings like all men, and that He can sympathize with their wants, and enter into their sorrows, although He is also the Son of God; that He is human as well as divine, — God in human flesh.

Q. Jesus, then, being the sower of the good seed, in what field does He sow it?

A. In the world (verse 33), — that is, in the hearts of mankind.

Q. We saw just now that the "good seed" stood in the parable for the good instructions, or good principles, that Jesus *sowed* in human hearts; but here, in order to explain himself further, He changed His interpretation a little; what does He put the good seed to signify *here*?

A. "The children of the kingdom"; that is, not only the good instructions of the gospel, but those individuals whose characters are *made Christian by these instructions*, and thus made children, or members, of His Kingdom, or Church.

Q. Are not all those who live as Jesus taught us to live, being baptized and repenting, "children of His kingdom," and members of His Church?

A. They are. See Catechism.

Q. Who are meant by the "tares"?

A. "The children of the wicked one" (verse 38).

Q. Who are these?

A. They are Satan's servants; persons who act on bad principles, lead wicked lives, and do not love and follow Jesus Christ.

Q. What is meant by the "devil" that makes us wicked, or that sows wicked impulses in our hearts?

A. The word "devil" means *adversary*; sin is always an *adversary* to our souls, the *enemy* of all our best interests, the *destroyer* of our peace and happiness.

Q. What do you understand by the phrase, "the reapers are the angels"?

A. At the harvest there are always reapers; and at this "harvest at the end of the world," when good and bad persons are to be gathered together, like sheaves of grain, at the last judgment, those who gather them will be the *angels*, that is, the *messengers* of God. These angels are "His," that is, Christ's, — who has all the power and authority of God.

Q. In verses 40-42, we are told what will become of the wicked; why is their future misery described by the Saviour as like that of being burned in "a furnace of fire"?

A. Because the remorse and shame they will suffer is like the anguish of fire burning the body; and this image was naturally suggested by his having just said that the *tares* (which stood for the wicked) were cast into the fire.

Q. What do you understand from the expression, "there shall be wailing and gnashing of teeth"?

A. That as these are the actions of persons suffering great pain, so will the wicked manifest their anguish when they look back on their sins against their Heavenly Father.

Q. But, on the other hand, what will be the condition of the good and the righteous at that great "harvest"?

A. They will "shine forth as the sun," be full of joy and brightness of spirit, under the approving smile of their Father in heaven.

Q. What do you learn, on the whole, from this parable?

A. First, that here on earth we must expect that the good and evil will dwell together; that the Church will have to live in a wicked world, and that there will be wicked men in the Church.

Q. But what do you learn beside?

A. That there must come a time of retribution, — a spiritual "harvest-time," — when the wicked will be visibly separated from the good; when the sinful will see their sin, in fruitless sorrow, and suffer for it; and when the good will find new joy and a glorious life.

Q. When you die, how will all your sins appear?

A. It will fill me with bitter anguish to think of them.

Q. What must be true of every sin you commit?

A. It hinders my Christian growth, corrupts the purity of my soul, and prepares suffering for me which I shall be sure to feel at the judgment of God.

LESSON VII.

PARABLE OF THE MUSTARD-SEED.

Q. Where is this parable recorded?

A. In St. Mark iv. 30–32; also in St. Luke xiii. 18, 19; and in St. Matthew xiii. 31, 32.

Q. Will you repeat it as it stands in St. Mark.

Q. If the disciples should be discouraged by the two former parables, how would this affect them?

A. It would cheer and comfort them.

Q. What other passage shows that the mustard-seed here spoken of by Jesus was small?

A. From St. Matt. xvii. 20, we should infer that it was so spoken of proverbially.

Q. If it grew to be so large as it is described in verse 32, must it not have been a different kind of mustard from any now known among us?

A. Travellers state that it was. One speaks of riding on horseback under the branches, and another mentions that the birds light on the boughs in large flocks to eat off the seeds.

Q. Do we find accounts in other books of a kind of mustard so large as this?

A. There are accounts of a shrub of this name, growing in the eastern countries, which bears a very small seed, but which lives several years, and grows so high that a man can climb up among the branches.

Q. Jesus compares to this mustard-seed the "Kingdom of God" (verse 30); what does He here mean by this?

A. The Church of God, as a spiritual power.

Q. How is the truth of this comparison exemplified?

A. In the spread of the gospel over the earth.

Q. How did the gospel begin?

A. Jesus, a despised carpenter from the little village of Nazareth, was at first its only teacher.

Q. Who followed him?

A. Twelve humble men, from obscure places, and but slightly educated, went forth as his Apostles to preach this religion, and they were everywhere spoken against, persecuted, and treated with contempt.

Q. What would a person looking on, at that time, naturally say that this new religion was like?

A. It must have appeared so feeble and unlike to live, that he might well have compared it to the little seed.

Q. But what happened soon?

A. This Faith was preached by these twelve men in various cities, great multitudes of people went to hear them, and believed them, and became Christians, and the Church arose in her living grandeur on the earth.

Q. In the course of a few years, what became true?

A. Not only large numbers were attached to the Christian faith, but among them were some of the most enlightened and powerful of the earth.

Q. How did it turn out in the course of a few centuries?

A. All the most important nations in the world were nations where this Christian Church was firmly established. (See Daniel ii. 34, 35.)

Q. At this day, are those nations that are not converted to Christianity to be compared in knowledge and power with the rest of the world?

A. They are not.

Q. What are these nations called, and where are they found?

A. They are called heathens, or pagans; and they are found principally in Africa, Asia, and some distant parts of America.

Q. If, then, the Christian religion has gone on overspreading the earth more and more with its light and its love, is it not very much like that mustard-seed that our Lord describes in the parable?

A. It is, and we see the appropriateness of the comparison.

Q. How did the Saviour know, — since His Church, when He spoke, had made scarcely any progress, — that it was destined to this wonderful success?

A. He had a Divine foreknowledge, and He saw beforehand what would happen after He should be taken up from the earth.

Q. How does our Lord say that His death and atonement will accomplish this?

A. St. John xii. 24.

Q. What ought to be our feeling when we consider this glorious progress that Christianity has made?

A. We should be very thankful to God that His providence has so ordered it.

Q. Why, especially?

A. Because this Faith saves the soul from sin, elevates men's characters, increases their wisdom, and makes them better and happier in a thousand ways.

Q. How shall we be most struck with this fact?

A. By looking at the vicious, ignorant, and degraded state of all heathen nations.

Q. How should we feel towards these heathens?

A. We should pity them, send out missionaries to them, and use all the means in our power to make them Christians.

Q. What *personal* reasons for gratitude have you?

A. I should be very thankful that I was born and live among Christian people, and enjoy Christian privileges, and not among the pagans, who worship images of wood and stone, or the sun and moon.

Q. But, having these superior advantages, what ought you to be in consequence of them?

A. I ought to be as much holier in my life, as my opportunities are better, a growing member of this growing Church.

Q. Why is the Church to her children like the mustard-tree to the birds?

A. She shelters and feeds them.

Q. Can you not give this parable an application to your own improvement in goodness?

A. I can; and it certainly teaches me that *my* faith and *my* goodness ought to increase daily, as the mustard-seed grew in size.

Q. How was Jesus an example for *you* and all children in this respect?

A. I read in Luke ii. 52, that, when He was about twelve years old, He increased not only in " stature," or in size, but also in " wisdom," and, by his Holiness, " in favor with God and man."

Q. How only can you thus grow?

A. By having Christ formed within me.

LESSON VIII.

PARABLE OF THE LEAVEN.

Q. What is " leaven " ?

A. It is the substance used in raising dough for bread, commonly called yeast.

Q. Where do you find the parable in which Jesus compares the kingdom of heaven, or the kingdom of God, to this leaven?

A. St. Luke writes it in his Gospel, in chap. xiii. 20, 21, and St. Matthew, in chap. xiii. 33.

Q. What do you infer from the fact that St. Luke says Jesus compared *the kingdom of God* to the leaven, while St. Matthew says that He compared *the kingdom of heaven* to the leaven?

A. That those two expressions, "the kingdom of God," and "the kingdom of heaven," mean the same thing, and may be used for each other.

Q. What may we take either and both of them to mean in this case?

A. The Church of Christ, with the Gospel doctrine, ministry, creed, sacraments, and worship, which He appointed and gave her.

Q. What is the Gospel?

A. The message Christ brought, from God the Father, into this world, showing us how we may be saved from sin.

LESSONS ON THE PARABLES. 37

Q. What is the meaning of " doctrine " ?

A. Doctrine means *something taught;* and a doctrine of the gospel is *something that Christ taught in His gospel,* or His message to mankind.

Q. In what other passages do we find *doctrine,* or *teachings,* compared to leaven ?

A. In St. Matthew xvi. 6, 12.

Q. Jesus speaks of the leaven as being put into three measures of meal ; how much were *three measures* ?

A. One measure was a peck and a half; three measures were four pecks and a half.

Q. Why does he mention this quantity ?

A. Because it was the quantity commonly used at once for making bread.

Q. How was bread baked among the Jews ?

A. Sometimes in the ashes (see 1 Kings xix. 6), sometimes on the hearth (see Gen. xviii. 6), and also in ovens, made probably of stones, and not resembling ours (see Lev. ii. 4).

Q. When yeast, or leaven, is placed in the dough that is made of meal, or flour, how does it operate ?

A. The yeast spreads and diffuses its influence through the whole mass of dough, till it *raises* it, or *makes it light.* (See 1 Cor. v. 6.)

Q. How is it that the gospel is like this leaven?

A. When once it has been made known to the minds of mankind, it goes on spreading itself more and more, and changing the lives of multitudes of people.

Q. Had this happened when Jesus spoke these words?

A. It had not, for He had preached the gospel in but few places, and but few persons, comparatively, had heard of it.

Q. How, then, could He say what He does in this parable ?

A. He was a prophet, and knew what would happen after He should have departed from the earth, namely, that His truth would be believed, and His life be imitated, more and more, as long as the world should stand.

Q. Has this proved true, so far, in history?

A. It has.

Q. How much time has passed since the Saviour departed from the earth?

A. More than eighteen hundred years.

Q. And has His gospel been spreading through all this period?

A. On the whole, it has; and by the efforts of Christians, and the blessing of God, some are brought to believe and obey it continually.

Q. What is there for us to do in the matter?

A. To try in every way to make Christ known and loved.

Q. How can we do so?

A. By being faithful to Him, and showing others what a noble and beautiful thing it is to follow Him.

Q. In what other way may we forward this object?

A. By embracing every good opportunity to help in giving religious instruction to the ignorant and the sinful.

Q. We have gained, then, one clear explanation of this parable; will you state it in one sentence?

A. As a little leaven *raises* a large mass of meal, so does the Christian faith spread from one heart to another, and from one nation to another, till it changes the life of mankind, and purifies, reforms, and saves the world.

Q. A piece of bread, or dough, is often used as leaven to make more bread; what does this suggest?

A. That it is by receiving Christ into the heart that the Christian becomes Christ-like.

Q. What other lesson may you practically learn from this parable?

A. That the gospel was meant to operate in any individual's character as it does in the world at large, — namely, to renew it, to change it more and more perfectly from evil to good, till the character is made thoroughly Christian.

Q. Should we ever be satisfied till this has taken place?

A. If we were, we should be spiritually dead.

Q. What is one thing about yourself that you should seek to have imbued with a Christian spirit, and governed by Christian principles?

A. My manner to those about me every day, making it gentle.

Q. What is another?

A. My disposition, making me generous and amiable.

Q. What is another?

A. My conversation, making it free from falsehood, slander, or profanity.

Q. How should your faith in Christ make you feel and act towards your parents?

A. To love, honor, and succor them, and seek to please them.

Q. When you are called on to transact business, what should it make your actions in that respect?

A. Honest, upright, and fair.

Q. How should it make you feel towards the sick, the poor, the oppressed, and the afflicted?

A. It should prompt me to pity them, and be ready to help them.

Q. How should it dispose you towards Jesus Christ?

A. It should make me very thankful that He came

from heaven for me; that He suffered in order to draw men to believe on Him, and to deliver them from sin; and it should fill me with a resolute desire to serve Him.

Q. How should it make you feel towards God your Heavenly Father?

A. It should make me thankful to Him for sending His Son to be the Saviour of men, and for all His spiritual mercies to me and my friends; and it should lead me to love Him, and endeavor to please Him, by doing His will all the days of my life.

LESSON IX.

PARABLES OF THE TREASURE IN A FIELD, AND OF THE PEARL OF GREAT PRICE.

Q. Will you repeat St. Matt. xiii. 44, containing the parable of the treasure hid in a field?

Q. What was probably meant by this " treasure "?

A. Silver or some other precious metal or precious stone, concealed under the ground.

Q. How do this and the next parable differ from the last two?

A. They relate to the Church as a whole; these to each member of it in his own seeking and finding.

Q. When the man had discovered that there was such a treasure in a field which was not his own, what is he represented as doing?

A. Hiding it.

Q. How did he " hide " it?

A. The meaning is that he kept it concealed, or

rather he kept his knowledge of it concealed, and did not tell others that it was there.

Q. What is meant by the expression, "for the joy thereof"?

A. In the joy that he felt at the prospect of gaining possession of so much wealth.

Q. What means did he take to get possession of it?

A. He bought the whole field where the treasure was.

Q. Why did he *sell all that he had*?

A. To provide himself with money sufficient to purchase the field.

Q. Suppose he had told the owner of the field his reason for wishing to buy it, or had offered to buy the treasure by itself, is it probable the owner would have parted with it as he did?

A. It is not; but being ignorant of the value of what was in his land, he sold it for less than it was worth.

Q. Does Jesus imply that it was right for this man to keep back what he knew for the sake of making a good bargain, and taking advantage of the owner?

A. He does not; on the contrary, we know from the whole strain of His teachings, and from the perfect justice and fairness of all His actions, that He would look upon such a transaction with abhorrence, as being dishonest and base.

Q. What, then, does He intend to teach by this comparison?

A. That the gospel is more precious than silver or gold; and that we ought to be more anxious to have it in our hearts than men of business are to secure a fortune.

Q. What is one of two facts, especially, that should

make us more eager to gain the goodness and truth of the gospel than earthly riches?

A. Goodness and truth last forever, and yield everlasting pleasure; while earthly riches perish, and are lost forever when we die.

Q. What is the other of these facts?

A. Goodness and truth are spiritual possessions, and therefore cannot fail to give us satisfaction; while earthly goods often bring as much trouble, anxiety, and sorrow, as enjoyment.

Q. Where are you to find this "goodness and truth"?

A. In my Saviour.

Q. Ought you ever to take advantage of another person's ignorance, to profit yourself at his expense?

A. Never; such an act is mean and contemptible.

Q. Suppose that, when you are buying an article of another person, you know of some circumstance about it which he does not know, but which, if he did know it, would make him ask a higher price for it, what ought you to do?

A. I ought to consider whether he has had fair means of knowing what I know; and if he has not, I ought to tell him, and then make my bargain afterwards, even though I should be obliged to pay more than if I had kept my secret.

Q. Suppose you had occasion to sell some article, and you knew of some circumstance about it which the buyer did not know, but which, if he did know it, would diminish the value of the article in his estimation, what ought you to do?

A. I ought to consider whether he has had fair means of knowing what I know, and if he has not, I ought to inform him, even though I should receive a smaller price from him in consequence.

Q. What may you say of those who pursue such conduct?

A. That they do business on noble and Christian principles.

Q. How do you learn that this high standard of dealing is correct?

A. My conscience, and the religion of Jesus, tell me that it is.

Q. What parable, having very much the same object with this one, is related in verses 45 and 46 of this chapter?

A. The parable of the pearl of great price.

Q. Is it meant that the "kingdom of heaven" is like the *man* seeking the pearls, or rather like the precious pearl itself?

A. It is like the pearl itself.

Q. What is a "pearl"?

A. It is a small ornament obtained from the shell of a kind of oyster, of a whitish color, and having a peculiar lustre.

Q. It seems that, in order to purchase this one "pearl of great price," the merchant was obliged to part with all his goods; how costly have pearls sometimes been?

A. There is an account of one which was purchased for about forty thousand dollars.

Q. Where have the most beautiful pearls been obtained?

A. In Arabia, and at the isle of Ceylon.

Q. What is said of the splendor of the New Jerusalem. — "Jerusalem the golden"?

A. Rev. xxi. 21.

Q. What does Jesus teach us by this parable?

A. That we ought to prize Him as infinitely more precious than the rarest pearl, or the costliest gem.

Q. What other passage of Scripture may this remind us of?

A. Proverbs iii. 13-15.

Q. What is meant by the "wisdom" spoken of there?

A. The wisdom which leads us to love God, and live a holy life.

Q. For what are we chiefly to prize the gospel?

A. Because it shows us the way from eternal death to eternal life, by the redemption of the cross; our Heavenly Father reveals to us how ready He is to forgive our sins when we repent; and teaches us how to be borne above all the evils of this world.

Q. What now, is the chief lesson you are to learn from these two parables?

A. That I ought never to prefer any thing else to the love of Jesus, or any place to my home in His Church.

Q. Suppose that you could not do your whole duty without denying yourself some pleasure that your heart was set upon, what would your duty be?

A. To deny myself that pleasure at once, and do my duty.

Q. What if you could gain money, or admiration, or some luxury, by doing wrong, — as by telling a falsehood, or disobeying your parents?

A. I ought to scorn to purchase either wealth, or the favor of other people, at that wicked price.

Q. When any thing else comes into conflict with the life of Christ, so that you must choose one or the other, what should your choice be?

A. To follow Him, which is always safe and good, however great the sacrifice it costs.

Q. How should you always value your membership in Christ?

A. Like the "treasure" and the "pearl" in the parables, so precious to my heart that I should be willing to part with all I have beside father than lose it.

LESSON X.

PARABLE OF THE NET.

Q. How many of the parables were probably delivered by Jesus on the same day?

A. The parable of the net, which seems to have been the last delivered on that day, makes eight.

Q. Will you repeat the circumstances under which Christ spoke these parables?

A. He was by the shore of the Sea of Galilee, sitting in a vessel, while the multitudes of people that He addressed were standing and listening to Him on the banks. (See St. Matt. xiii. 1, 2.)

Q. What is the first of these parables, and what does it teach?

A. The parable of the sower, which teaches how the doctrines of the gospel taught by the Church are received in the souls of different persons.

Q. What is the second, and what does it teach?

A. The parable of the tares, teaching us that though the good and the bad must live together on earth, yet there is a moral separation between them which must hereafter divide their souls, even as the wheat is gathered into barns, but the tares are burned up with fire.

Q. What is the third, and its lesson?

A. The parable of the growing grain, which shows that we must take the gospel earnestly into our hearts, in order that it may grow in us and gradually change our lives, and bear the fruit of good actions. (See Lesson xi.)

Q. What is the fourth, and its lesson?

A. The parable of the mustard-seed, which illustrates the *progressive* nature of Christianity, or how, from small beginnings, it reaches great results in improving the character, and converting the world.

Q. What is the fifth, and what does it teach?

A. The parable of the leaven, which shows the *diffusive* nature of our Christian faith, and how it spreads through the heart, or through the community where it is welcomed.

Q. What are the sixth and seventh, and their lesson?

A. The parables of the treasure in the field, and of the pearl of great price, teaching us the unspeakable worth and preciousness of Christ's truth, and its superiority over every other possession.

Q. What, now, is the eighth, and what does it show?

A. The parable of the net, which shows, like the parable of the tares, that though there will be gathered into the Church on earth both good and bad, yet that these must finally be separated, and only the good enter heaven. (See St. Matt. xiii. 47–50.)

Q. Can you think of any circumstance that should have suggested to the mind of Jesus this parable concerning a net and fishing?

A. He was speaking in a vessel, which was, very likely, a fishing-vessel, on a sea where many fish were caught, and perhaps within sight of nets spread out to be dried.

Q. What should we learn from this custom of our Lord, of drawing out religious lessons from common events and familiar objects?

A. To make such things remind *us* of our duties and our spiritual life.

Q. Looking at this parable of the net, what would naturally happen if a net were dragged through the water, as described in verse 47?

A. It would gather into it various sorts of fish, — large and small, good and bad, and bring them all to the shore together.

Q. What kinds of nets were used by the fishermen of Galilee?

A. Two kinds, "casting nets," and "draw nets." Christ uses a Greek word meaning the draw net, so large as take in many kinds of fish. It is sometimes half a mile long.

Q. What fish did the Jews consider "bad"?

A. See Leviticus xi. 9–12.

Q. What is done when these fish of various kinds are brought to land?

A. See verse 48.

Q. What are these fish then compared to (verse 49)?

A. To those persons, good and bad, who belong, or pretend to belong, to the company of Christian believers.

Q. What will happen at last, when God shall send forth His messengers?

A. The wicked shall be separated from the good, and while the good are made happy in their holiness, the wicked will be made miserable by their sins.

Q. What is that feeling which makes a bad child, or a bad man, miserable, when he looks back on the sins he has committed, in his words, and thoughts, and conduct?

A. The accusation of his conscience, or remorse.

Q. Why is one who is suffering this inward torment said to be "cast into a furnace of fire"?

A. Because his sufferings will be such as we cannot fully conceive of now, and will be like the torment of being burned alive.

Q. Were persons actually burned in those days?

A. Persons guilty of great crimes were burned, as their punishment.

Q. What do you understand by verse 50?

A. It is descriptive of those horrible agonies which sin must some time bring upon the guilty soul.

Q. After Jesus had finished these parables, what question did He put to those who had listened to them?

A. See verse 51.

Q. And what did they reply?

A. See verse 51.

Q. What meaning has the word "scribe" in verse 52?

A. It means "scholar."

Q. What is meant by the phrase, "instructed unto the kingdom of heaven"?

A. "Instructed to know what the Church of Christ is, and what the gospel contains," as these parables had shown.

Q. What does Jesus say that a Christian who knows this is like?

A. See verse 52.

Q. Why is he like this householder?

A. Because he is thoroughly furnished with spiritual knowledge, as the householder is with earthly treasures.

Q. What does the parable signify as to being in the Church on earth?

A. That it is our place, and a blessed place; but that

there may be bad people in it, as there was bad fish in the net, their hearts still selfish and unholy.

Q. What did Jesus do after 'He had spoken all these beautiful instructions to the people?

A. (See verse 53.)

LESSON XI.

PARABLE OF THE GROWING GRAIN.

Q. If you had been standing by the shore of the Sea of Galilee, in Palestine, one day near the close of Christ's life on earth, what might you have seen there?

A. A multitude of people, of all ranks and ages, gathered in one spot, in the open air, and listening attentively to a teacher who was addressing them with wonderful earnestness.

Q. Who was this teacher?

A. Jesus, the Son of God, the Saviour of men.

Q. On what subjects did He speak?

A. He spoke to those who heard Him of their Father in heaven, of their higher duties, their spiritual natures, and of the life which their souls should live after death.

Q. What may you say of these subjects?

A. They are the most interesting, and the most sublime, that can possibly engage our attention.

Q. How did the Saviour speak of them?

A. He spake, we are told, "as never man spake;" and we know that none has spoken like him since.

Q. Why was this?

A. He came into the world, "God manifest in the flesh," that the world might believe Him, trust Him, and learn from Him how to be holy.

Q. Do not His teachings strike us, of themselves, as true and good?

A. They do; something in our own hearts seems to assure us, that what He said must be true, and designed to make us better.

Q. What is another circumstance that makes us confide in Christ and believe on Him?

A. The fact that He lived Himself just as he taught us to live, and practiced the virtues which He told us to practice.

Q. How does it affect us to see a teacher whose daily conduct is not consistent with his good instructions?

A. It takes away our confidence in him, because it leaves us to suspect that he is not sincere in what he says.

Q. If good persons loved to gather about Jesus and *hear* Him teach when He was on earth, how will good children feel about reading and studying what He said, as it is written in the New Testament?

A. They will love to do so, and they will be eager to understand the meaning of His words, and treasure them up in their memory.

Q. Where do you find this parable of the growing grain?

A. It is omitted by St. Luke and St. Matthew, but it is recorded by St. Mark iv. 26–29.

Q. When His instructions have been received into the heart of a man, what does Christ say they are like?

A. Like seed planted in a good soil.

Q. What does Jesus say happens to such seed?

A. It swells, takes root, sends up a green shoot above the surface, and gradually grows till it reaches its full size and bears fruit.

Q. While all this is taking place, has the man who sowed it any thing farther to do with it?

A. He has not; it grows, under the care of God's providence, without any farther help from him (verse 27).

Q. What mistake is made by some Christians?

A. They think too much of themselves, or *how* the seed grows in them, instead of looking away to Christ and taking hold of His work among men.

Q. When Jesus describes the process of the grain's growing (verse 28), what does He mean by the "blade"?

A. The green shoot that appears first when the grain rises above the ground.

Q. What is the "ear"?

A. That part of the wheat that forms on the top of the blade, or stalk, to contain the fruit.

Q. What is the "full corn in the ear"?

A. The kernels of grain that ripen just before the harvest, and of which the flour is made for bread.

Q. When this is ripe, what does the husbandman do?

A. See verse 29. He both *sows* and *reaps*, but in the interval he can do nothing to mature his crop.

Q. What seems to have been the object of Jesus in this parable?

A. To show His disciples that the work of Christian truth in forming a good character is *gradual;* that it is not all done at once, but that it goes on by successive stages, as wheat grows, until the character is completely formed.

Q. What, then, are we to remember is of the greatest importance?

A. That we make our hearts like the good soil, and really receive into them the holy principles of our religion.

Q. If we do not heartily receive them, and thoroughly believe them, will they bring forth fruit, and make us Christians?

A. They will not, any more than that soil will bear a harvest which is so hard that the seed does not sink into it.

Q. When does the Christian life *begin*?

A. When God's grace first plants it in the soul.

Q. If we have never passed through this change how can we hope to gain it?

A. By forsaking our sins, striving continually to be holy, and praying to our Father in heaven to help us.

Q. Then, being baptized, having begun to be Christians, what does this parable teach us to do next?

A. To go on, to persevere, to grow better and better every day, with the helps of the Church.

Q. How does the comparison of the grain apply?

A. As the grain is ever growing higher and more perfect, so should we be ever growing purer, wiser, and holier. (See Heb. vi. 1; 2 Pet. i. 5–7.)

Q. In what respects, particularly, ought our characters to exhibit this *progress*?

A. In our growing more and more humble, more and more truthful and sincere, more and more self-denying, gentle, obedient, and devout.

Q. If, after having pretended to begin the Christian life, we miserably forsake it, and go back to sinful habits, what shall we show?

A. That we did not really take the purpose deeply into our hearts, nor strive earnestly enough to follow Christ.

Q. What should be our continual aim and endeavor?

A. That as long as we live we may never cease to grow more and more like our Master and Saviour.

Q. If this is our course, what may we hope for, at that great "harvest" when we shall all rise from the dead and appear before God?

A. That He will welcome us to His presence, and permit us to grow holier and happier in an everlasting life.

LESSON XII.

PARABLE OF THE BREAD.

Q. WHAT wonderful work of the Saviour is recorded in the first part of the sixth chapter of John's Gospel?

A. The miracle by which He fed five thousand persons with five loaves of bread and two fishes.

Q. Where was this miracle performed?

A. On the northern shore of the Sea of Galilee, near a city called Bethsaida. (See map, and also St. Luke ix. 10.)

Q. How was Jesus occupied there?

A. (See St. Luke ix. 11.)

Q. Where had He been, just before this?

A. On the western shore of the Sea of Galilee, near Nazareth.

Q. What do we learn that Jesus did the night after He performed this miracle?

A. (See St. John, chap. vi., from verse 16 to verse 21.)

Q. Where then was He on the following day?

A. At or near Capernaum.

Q. What direction must He have taken to pass from Bethsaida to Capernaum?

A. (See map.)

Q. Did the multitude follow after Him?

A. (See verses 22–25.)

Q. What motive did Jesus accuse them of (verse 26) in following Him?

A. Of a desire to obtain food for the body.

Q. What admonition does He give them in verse 27?

A. That they should be less anxious to gratify their earthly appetites than to gain His truth, which is the bread of the mind.

Q. What does He tell them this spiritual truth, which is the nourishment of the soul, will do for them?

A. It will give them everlasting life, as what is eaten for food supports, in the body, its earthly life.

Q. How does He say we may obtain this truth to nourish our souls?

A. By believing on Him, the Saviour, and obeying His words: for His Father in heaven had " sealed," or sent Him, that He might teach and save us.

Q. When the people ask Him (verse 28) what works they shall do that will be pleasing to God, what does He reply?

A. That they should believe on Him whom God sent to be their Saviour, even Jesus Christ.

Q. If we really heartily believe in Christ, shall we not obey His precepts?

A. We must.

Q. And if we do this, what will His doctrines be?

A. Like bread to the body, giving life and energy to our souls in this world and after our bodies are dead.

Q. What did these people allude to, when they said, "Our fathers did eat manna in the desert"?

A. To the fact that their ancestors, the Israelites, lived on manna when they were travelling through the wilderness from Egypt to Palestine. (See Exodus xvi.)

Q. What does Jesus say of this manna, and of Moses, who was the leader of those Israelites when they received it?

A. That Moses did not give them the *true bread* from heaven, either in manna or in his laws.

Q. What, then, is the *true bread* from heaven?

A. It is Christ (verse 33).

Q. When the people ask Him to give them that bread, what does He answer?

A. That He *does* give it to them, because He gives *Himself* to make them good, and *He* is that bread.

Q. What do you understand by the figurative language in verse 35?

A. That as the body, when it has eaten and drunk enough, feels no more hunger or thirst, so whoever takes Jesus for his heart, will not feel any inward want, but will be satisfied.

Q. What is the only thing that can really satisfy our souls?

A. Christ.

Q. How did the Jews mistake the meaning of Jesus (verses 41, 42) when He said He came down from heaven?

A. They supposed He meant that He bodily came down from above the sky, while He really meant that His Divine nature came and took up our human nature.

Q. Where does He repeat what He had just said, and enlarge upon it?

A. In verses 48 to 58.

Q. What is the meaning of verses 49 and 50?

A. That manna and bread support the body only for a time, but cannot prevent its dying at last; while the soul that loves and follows Christ never dies, but lives on in glory after the body has decayed.

Q. What are we to understand when Jesus says (verse 51) that He gives His flesh for the life of the world?

A. That He devoted all His life and at last died on the cross to take away their spiritual death, and that they might live on Him.

Q. But how does it appear that *you* will live forever, — that *your* life will be eternal, — if you are good?

A. Because then I shall have Christ my Life living in me, and can never perish.

Q. What, then, should be your grand object now?

A. Not so much to provide bodily comforts, as to "lay hold on eternal life," in Jesus Christ.

Q. How do we eat of our Lord's flesh in the Holy Sacrament?

A. St. Luke xxii. 19 ; I. Cor. x. 16, 17.

Q. Why, then, should you and all Christians seek and prize the Communion of the Lord's Supper?

A. Because it is the Christian's special privilege and help, a divine means of coming near to Christ, partaking of Him, and receiving the rich gift of His Spirit and His Life, if only the communicant has "a true penitent heart and lively faith."

LESSON XIII.

PARABLE OF THE UNFORGIVING SERVANT.

Q. For what purpose did the Saviour give the parable of the unforgiving servant?

A. To teach His followers that they should forgive all those that injure them.

Q. What is the great reason set forth here for our forgiving injuries?

A. The fact that we must depend on the forgiveness of our Father in heaven, to have eternal life and peace of heart.

Q. Why is this?

A. We have all sinned, and nothing but the forgiveness of God can relieve us from the miserable punishment of our sins.

Q. If we would hope, then, to be forgiven, what must we first do?

A. We must forgive others.

Q. Is not this plainly implied in one of the petitions of the Lord's Prayer?

A. "Forgive us our trespasses, as we forgive them that trespass against us."

Q. In what passages of the Sermon on the Mount is the same thing declared?

A. In St. Matt. vi. 14, 15, and v. 7.

Q. In what other part of Christ's instructions do you find a passage resembling this parable?

A. In St. Luke vii. 41-43.

Q. Where is the parable itself recorded?

A. In St. Matt. xviii. 23, and the remaining verses of the chapter.

Q. What drew this parable from Him at this time?

A. The question asked by St. Peter, one of the Apostles (verse 21).

Q. What is the meaning of Christ's answer to that question, in verse 22?

A. That we should forgive our fellow-creatures, not exactly four hundred and ninety times, but *any number of times,* — an indefinite number, — as often as they offend against us.

Q. How does Jesus explain and enforce His meaning?

A. By supposing a case, and telling the story of a servant who was forgiven, but who would not forgive.

Q. When the king, in the story, reckons with his servants, how much is one of them found to owe him?

A. "Ten thousand talents,"— an immense sum of money, amounting to millions of dollars.

Q. How would a servant be likely to owe the king so vast a debt?

A. He was not probably a *household* servant, but a prince or ruler of a station inferior to that of the king, and yet having large dealings with him.

Q. When this servant was found quite unable to pay his debt, what did the king command to be done, in order that his demand might be satisfied?

A. (Verse 25.)

Q. Was it customary among the Jews to sell persons into servitude to pay their debts?

A. It was. (See Lev. xxv. 39–41, 47; 2 Kings iv. 1.)

Q. What is meant when it is said that the servant fell down and *worshiped* the king?

A. That he prostrated himself, with great humility and deference, not that he offered that *worship* which is due to God alone.

Q. When the servant made his earnest appeal to the king, that he might be exempted from this fate, and suffered to be at liberty till he could repay the money, what did the king do?

A. (Verse 27.)

Q. What base and mean thing was this servant immediately guilty of?

A. (Verses 28–30.)

Q. What makes his conduct appear doubly disgraceful?

A. The circumstance that he had just been treated with pity and mercy.

Q. How is this brought out with peculiar force?

A. The words used by his fellow-servant *without avail* are the very *same words* used by himself, which obtained the forbearance of the king.

Q. What other circumstance still further aggravates the wickedness of this act?

A. While the servant had just been released from a debt of millions of dollars, he would not release his fellow-servant who was under a debt of only about fourteen dollars.

Q. What was the value of a "penny" among the Jews?

A. A penny, or denarius, was worth about fourteen of our cents.

Q. After the servant had cruelly and ungratefully cast his fellow-debtor into prison, what happened?

A. (Verse 31.)

Q. What did the king say to the servant?

A. (Verses 32, 33.)

Q. Does it appear that the servant had any thing to answer to this rebuke?

A. He had nothing.

Q. What then did the king do, to punish such outrageous ingratitude and cruelty?

A. (Verse 34.) He delivered him to the "tormentors," — that is, to the jail-keepers, — who sometimes increased the punishment of prisoners by torturing them with whips, or chains, or partial starvation.

Q. Where do we find the application of this parable?

A. In verse 35.

Q. Who is represented to us by the "king"?

A. God, the Creator and Ruler of the universe, to whom we are all accountable.

Q. Who is represented by the "servant"?

A. Any human being, — any one of us.

Q. If you were that servant, who would your "fellow-servants" be?

A. All human beings, — members of the great human family.

Q. What is the "debt" spoken of, which we owe to God?

A. That debt that is created by our sins against Him, or against His commands; for our obedience belongs to Him.

Q. Have we not full assurance that our Father loves us so tenderly, that He is willing to forgive us whenever we repent of our sins?

A. We have, both in His word, and in the fact that He gave his dear Son to suffer and die to deliver us from our sins, and bring us to repentance and salvation.

Q. If, then, every sin we commit puts us in debt towards God, since we sin every day, how great must this debt be?

A. Larger than we can conceive, and infinitely larger than the amount of any one's offenses towards *us*.

Q. And if our Father is willing to forgive such an enormous amount of evil in us the moment we repent and forsake it, how should we feel toward the evil that we see in our fellow-mortals?

A. We should be not only ready, but eager, to pardon it, and try to forget it.

Q. When some of your companions have been unjust, or overbearing, or peevish, or ill-natured, — when they have ridiculed you, or provoked you, or slandered you, — what should you seek first of all things to do?

A. To forgive them entirely, from my very heart.

Q. When a person says that he can *forgive* an injury, but that he cannot *forget* it, what may you generally infer?

A. That he does not *really, thoroughly* forgive it.

Q. What three high motives especially urge you to forgive all who vex or injure you in any way?

A. I should do so because my conscience will be peaceful and happy after it; because Jesus Christ, who is my example, did so (see Luke xxiii. 33, 34); and because I may then hope that my many sins will be forgiven by my Father in heaven.

Q. How is forgiveness connected with love?
A. (See St. Luke vii. 41–50.)

LESSON XIV.

PARABLE OF THE LABORERS IN THE VINEYARD.

Q. How will you learn the object and meaning of the parable of the laborers in the vineyard, as it is recorded in St. Matt. xx. 1–16?

A. By reading what Jesus had just been saying, in the latter part of chap. xix., and especially in the last verse.

Q. What is the meaning of that verse?

A. That many who should afterwards become believers of the gospel would enter more fully into its spirit, and therefore share more largely in its rewards, than those, like the Jews, who outwardly professed it at an early date.

Q. What shows particularly that Jesus designed to illustrate this truth by this parable?

A. The word "for," at the beginning of verse 1 of chap. xx., connecting this passage with what goes before.

Q. How may we vary the reading of the first verse?

A. So as to make it, — "God, in His method of receiving mankind into the kingdom of heaven, is like," &c.

Q. Jesus then goes on to compare the Creator to a certain householder. Who are represented by the laborers that he hired to work in his vineyard?

A. Those persons who are invited to come and labor, as disciples of Jesus Christ, in works of Christian faith.

Q. Why is a "vineyard" mentioned here?

A. Cultivating grapes was a common occupation among the Jews; and a garden or field stocked with the vines was called a "vineyard."

Q. What is the sum mentioned in verse 2 as a day's wages?

A. A penny, or about fourteen cents, the usual price at that time and in that country.

Q. When was the "third hour"?

A. Among the Jews and Romans, the day began at six o'clock, A. M., and the hour from six to seven was called the *first* hour; the third hour would be that completed at nine o'clock, A. M.

Q. The householder hired other laborers at the sixth, and others still at the ninth hour (verse 5); what would those hours be in our reckoning?

A. As we just saw, the sixth would reach to twelve o'clock at noon, and the ninth to three o'clock, P. M.

Q. When was the last set of laborers hired?

A. At about the eleventh hour, or between four and five o'clock in the afternoon.

Q. At the close of the day's work the owner bade his steward pay the laborers; what was the office of this "steward"?

A. To oversee the affairs of the household. (See the Lesson on the Parable of the Unjust Steward.)

Q. Why did the householder order a full day's wages to be given to those who only began to work at four or five o'clock?

A. Perhaps because he saw that they worked more strenuously and faithfully or in a better spirit than the others who began in the morning; perhaps because he pitied their condition in that they were *not able* to obtain work and wages through the day.

Q. What complaint was made by those who had labored all the day?

A. That their fellows should receive equal pay, with less work.

Q. But did they not receive that for which they fairly "agreed," as appears from verse 2?

A. They did; and therefore they had no right to complain. All were rewarded.

Q. Was it not a small jealousy in them to be irritated because the householder chose to be liberal to their companions, as long as he was perfectly just to them?

A. It appears so from his unanswerable words in verses 13-15.

Q. What is the signification of the expression (verse 15), "Is thine eye evil because I am good?"

A. "Should you feel the bad passion of envy or selfishness because I choose to be generous?"

Q. At the conclusion of the parable, Jesus repeats the declaration that He made at the beginning; will you state the meaning of this verse 16?

A. Those who shall learn the Christian doctrine as soon as they can shall not suffer because they had not the means of learning it sooner; that is rather their misfortune than their fault.

Q. Had not Jesus here a distinct reference to the Jews and the Gentiles?

A. Probably He had, and meant to say, that many Gentiles (or persons of foreign nations), who might be converted to Christianity years after the Jews had heard of it, would yet hold a higher place in the scale of Christian excellence and joy, on account of their better dispositions and lives.

Q. What lesson may you learn from this parable?

A. I may learn to thank my Heavenly Father that He has shown this liberal and kind favor toward all His children alike; and that He blesses those who are true disciples of His Son, as much in one age of the world as in another.

Q. What other lesson may you learn?

A. To despise and shun every feeling of envy or malice toward those who seem to be more highly favored in any respect than myself.

Q. What is true of zealous and busy Christians who harbor pride, self-conceit, and uncharitableness in the midst of their works?

A. They will be less blessed than the really humble and holy who seem to accomplish less.

Q. What other lesson still, — the most important of all?

A. To embrace with all my heart the faith offered me by so kind a Father, and to follow carefully and cheerfully my holy Saviour.

Q. What is of more importance in our Lord's eyes than the quantity of our performances?

A. Our Christian spirit in doing it.

LESSON XV.

PARABLE OF THE GOOD SAMARITAN.

Q. WILL you repeat the parable of the good Samaritan?

A. (See the Gospel of St. Luke, chap. x. 30-38.)

Q. How do you learn what was the occasion of Christ's speaking this parable?

A. By referring to verse 25, and the following verses.

Q. What was this "lawyer" who questioned Jesus?

A. He was a person who gave himself to the study and explanation of the written laws of Moses, a "scribe."

Q. Were the scribes spoken of in the New Testament generally estimable characters?

A. They were often wanting in hearty feeling and sincere piety, being, like the Pharisees, more careful to insist on ceremonies, and repeat forms and words, than to serve God and love mankind.

Q. What is meant when it is said (verse 25) that this teacher of the law *tempted* Jesus?

A. That he put a question from a bad motive, namely, a desire to trouble Jesus, and if possible to make Him contradict himself.

Q. Did Jesus refuse to answer him?

A. He did not, but took pains to enlighten and improve him.

Q. Jesus tells this scribe (see verses 27 and 28) what it is necessary to do in order to gain eternal life; how then does the scribe raise another question?

A. By asking, "Who is my neighbor?" implying that, though it might be his duty to love his *neighbor*, he was not obliged to love all mankind.

Q. How does Christ make him acknowledge his mistake, and show him that he ought to love every man, even his enemy?

A. By relating to him the parable of the Good Samaritan.

Q. Jesus supposes a certain man to be going from Jerusalem to Jericho; what may have suggested to His thoughts these two places, and this particular journey, just at this time?

A. He may have been in that part of the country Himself.

Q. What reason have you for thinking so?

A. We find from other passages that He had just been travelling from Capernaum, through Samaria; from verse 38 of this chapter, we find that, soon after, He arrived at a certain village where Mary and Martha lived, and this village we know was Bethany. (See St. John xi. 1.)

Q. Will you point out Capernaum, and Samaria, and Jericho, and Bethany, on a map of Palestine?

Q. Jesus speaks of this man whom He imagines to be going from Jerusalem to Jericho as "falling among thieves"; what reason have we for believing this was likely to happen there?

A. Travellers who have been there tell us it is a very lonely district of country, full of wild mountains, which are infested with bands of thieves and robbers.

Q. A priest and a Levite are spoken of as passing by the poor man, after he had been robbed and was lying wounded and helpless, without assisting him; how would it naturally happen that priests and Levites should be often on that road?

A. A great many of them — twelve thousand, it is

said — lived in Jericho, but had frequent occasion to go up to Jerusalem, to perform ceremonies at the great Temple there.

Q. Who were the priests among the Jews, and what was their business?

A. They were the descendants of Aaron, and their business was to perform religious offices, to instruct the people in the law, to offer sacrifices on the altars, and to cleanse and take care of the Temple.

Q. Who were the Levites, and what was their business?

A. They were descendants of Levi; and they were set apart to wait on the priests, as their servants, in and about the temple, and sometimes to make music at worship.

Q. If these persons, then, were religious officers, was it not peculiarly their duty to aid the distressed, and minister to the suffering, like this poor traveller?

A. It was; and therefore their cruelty and hardness of heart in passing by him is the more blameworthy.

Q. Who was it that took pity on the wounded man?

A. It was a Samaritan, or man from Samaria.

Q. But the man he helped was a Jew; was there not a hatred between the Samaritans and the Jews?

A. There was. (See St. John iv. 9.)

Q. Seeing, then, that there was this hostility between the two nations, was it not very generous in the Samaritan to overlook the quarrel, and show compassion for the Jew?

A. It was this that made his act peculiarly praiseworthy in the eyes of Christ, and has drawn toward him the admiration of all good men who have ever read the story.

Q. Is it not always noble and generous to rise above our little injuries and hard feelings, and forgive our enemies?

A. Christ forgave even those who slandered Him and put Him to death; and He taught us to have the same spirit.

Q. If we are truly Christlike, what shall we do?

A. We shall pity and help one man as well as another, even strangers and foreigners.

Q. What did this Samaritan do for the poor Jew?

A. (Verses 33–35.)

Q. Why did he pour oil and wine upon the wounds?

A. A kind of ointment was made of these things that was healing.

Q. How much was the value of the "two pence" that he gave to the inn-keeper for taking care of the man?

A. About twenty-eight cents in the coin used at that time.

Q. Was not the law-teacher obliged to confess that this was true generosity?

A. He was, though his hatred of the very name of Samaritan was so strong that he would not speak it, but chose the expression " He that showed mercy on him" instead.

Q. From this parable, whom should we learn to regard as our neighbors, in the Christian sense?

A. Not those who happen to live near us only; but all of our fellow-creatures, for God has made us to sympathize with all.

> "Our neighbor is the suffering man,
> Though at the farthest pole."

Q. How are we to heed the precept with which Jesus concluded this parable,— " Go and do thou likewise "?

A. By endeavoring ourselves to perform kind offices for the distressed, and by feeling for others' troubles.

Q. What are some of the classes of persons that we ought especially to comfort?

A. The sick, the poor, the oppressed, orphans, and those that are in affliction.

Q. Ought we not to think it a privilege to share our own comforts with those who have not so many as we?

A. If we are truly humane, or truly Christians, we cannot do otherwise.

Q. If we are able to bestow few outward gifts, what can we, even the poorest, give?

A. Our prayers, kind words and actions, and our sympathy.

Q. If we follow the Saviour's pattern of benevolence, what shall we be ready to do for the unfortunate?

A. To lay aside our own wishes, and deny ourselves some pleasures, and incur some labor and inconvenience, for the sake of making them happy.

Q. What duty toward those who have injured or vexed you do you learn from this parable?

A. To treat them with compassion and generosity, as well as those that have befriended me. (St. Matt. v. 44, 45.)

Q. If you do this, whose approbation will you be sure to gain?

A. That of my merciful Heavenly Father, who is kind to me, notwithstanding my frequent offenses against Him. "He maketh His sun to rise on the evil and on the good; He sendeth rain on the just and on the unjust."

LESSON XVI.

PARABLE OF THE MAN AT REST AT NIGHT.

Q. Where do you find this parable?

A. In St. Luke's Gospel, chap. xi., verses 5–8.

Q. What was the object of Jesus in relating it?

A. To teach us to pray, and to continue in the habit of praying.

Q. What great motive does He offer us for frequent prayer?

A. He shows that sincere, earnest prayer will be answered.

Q. From the preceding verses of the chapter, we learn what occasion it was that drew from Christ this parable; what do we learn from verse 1?

A. That Jesus was in the habit of praying and communing with His Father, and that thus He was Himself an example of what He taught us to be. (See also St. Matt. xiv. 23; St. Luke vi. 12; ix. 28; St. Mark i. 35; xiv. 35; St. John xvii. 1, &c.)

Q. It is here that John the Baptist taught his disciples to pray. Was it customary in those times for religious teachers to instruct their followers, or disciples, in some particular form of prayer?

A. It was.

Q. After reciting the prayer which the Church was always to use, Christ relates this parable; how does it begin?

A. A person is supposed to be called up in the night by the arrival of a traveller, who wishes for a lodging and a supper.

Q. Is it customary for persons in the country of Judea, where Jesus was, to travel in the night?

A. It is, because the climate is extremely warm, and it is more comfortable to journey in the cool of the night than under the sun in the daytime.

Q. Being thus disturbed, the man of the house finds that he has no bread to offer the traveller; what does he do?

A. He goes to a neighbor, awakes him, and asks him to lend him three loaves.

Q. What reply does the neighbor make?

A. That both he and his children are in bed, and that he cannot easily rise to get the loaves.

Q. Is he finally prevailed upon to do so, however?

A. He is, by his friend's importunity; that is, by his repeating and urging the request.

Q. If, then, this neighbor could be persuaded to do what was asked by the urging of his friend, and not by any hearty desire to accommodate, is it not much more certain that our Heavenly Father, who tenderly loves us, will grant our requests when we pray to Him?

A. This is what Christ designs to teach us.

Q. How does He show this in verses 9 and 10?

A. He tells us there, in figurative language, that whatever we earnestly ask our Father in heaven to give us, for the good of our souls, He will surely bestow upon us.

Q. What does He tell us in the three following verses?

A. That as kind earthly parents, when the children they love ask them for good and reasonable gifts, do not put them off with worthless or hurtful ones, so our Heavenly Parent, whose love is yet stronger and purer, can never refuse to answer our petitions.

Q. What is meant by the expression, "Your Heavenly Father will give *the Holy Spirit* to them that ask Him "?

A. That He will give that Spirit to purify, and guide, and bless, and save our spirits.

Q. What is one of our chief dangers respecting this privilege of prayer?

A. That amidst our worldly occupations we shall forget and neglect it.

Q. Shall we not be greatly in fault if we do thus forget it?

A. We shall, for it depends on ourselves whether we allow ourselves to become so much engrossed with worldly things.

Q. How can we guard against this?

A. By setting apart some moments at a certain time, every day, for devotion.

Q. How should we spend such moments?

A. Going away alone, we should think seriously of our faults, and ask God to pity us and forgive us, and help us to amend our lives and to please Him.

Q. Has He not promised that He will forgive us and smile upon us, if we truly repent of our sins and ask His pardon?

A. He has, many times, in the New Testament. (See St. Luke vi. 37; 1 St. John i. 9.)

Q. What assistance should we especially entreat God to afford us?

A. His help in enabling us to resist those temptations to which each of us is especially exposed, so that we may not be turned aside from His way.

Q. If you feel that you are peculiarly in danger of doing wrong at some particular time, or in some particular way, what should you do to guard against it?

A. Pray God to help me and strengthen me, and make me to do right.

Q. What should you seek His assistance for, besides helping you to do right in your outward actions?

A. For controlling my language and conversation, so that I may speak nothing false, peevish, passionate, profane, slanderous, impure, or mean, and " offend not with my tongue."

Q. What else?

A. That He would aid me in keeping sin away from my secret thoughts and hidden feelings; because sin is as bad for me in secret as in public, and is just as offensive to Him " who seeth in secret."

Q. What is another important part of prayer?

A. Praying for others, which is called intercession.

Q. How should you pray for others?

A. I should ask God to bless them by making them good and happy, and sending them faith, hope, and peace.

Q. How can you pray for the interests of the truth?

A. By asking God to make every good cause prosperous, especially His holy Church, to spread knowledge, virtue, and piety over the whole earth, and to incline young men to seek the sacred office of the ministry.

Q. What classes of people do you feel that you should especially remember in your times of devotion?

A. The poor, the sick, the injured, the sorrowful, and, above all, the vicious.

Q. Ought you to pray for your enemies as well as your friends?

A. My Saviour tells me that I ought, St. Matt. v. 44, and He prayed, " Father, forgive them," for those who were putting Him to death on the cross.

Q. Will God make us good unless we try also to make ourselves good?

A. We have no promise that He will.

Q. What is a proper subject for your prayer?

A. Any thing and every thing that I seriously think of.

Q. What is yet another important part of devotion?

A. That we should thank our Father in heaven for all His kindness and mercy towards us His children every moment we live, for He gives us every good thing.

Q. When Jesus gives us the form of prayer mentioned in verses 2-4 of this chapter, and also in Matt. vi. 9, &c., does He intend that we shall always repeat this prayer and *only* this?

A. He does not; though He teaches us that we should pray *after this manner*, and *often* repeat this, for it is undoubtedly the most perfect of all prayers.

Q. If we should take up each one of the expressions in it, should we not find that they either include or suggest every thing that we ought to pray for?

A. We should, and we ought always to think earnestly of the meaning of what we utter in this and in all other prayers.

Q. When we hear others pray aloud what should we do?

A. We should follow the language, and endeavor to make the prayer our own, by entering into it, and feeling it with all our hearts, and therefore say "Amen."

Q. What are we particularly to remember, as the lesson of this parable?

A. That if we persevere faithfully in the habit of sincere prayer, God so loves us that He will hear us, and answer us.

Q. How do you know this?

A. God has promised it, though He does not tell us how or when the answer will come.

Q. But in whose name, or through whom must you pray?

A. Through Jesus Christ, except when I pray to Him, and with entire submission to His will, *i. e.* willing He shall do for me whatever He sees best.

LESSON XVII.

PARABLE OF THE MAN WITH MANY GOODS.

Q. Where is this parable recorded?

A. St. Luke xii. 16–21.

Q. What caused Christ to put forth this parable?

A. Some one came and asked that the family estate might be divided between his brother and himself, — probably with a desire to get really more than his share (verse 13).

Q. Why should he ask Jesus to make this division?

A. Because he perceived that Jesus had great authority, and that others would obey His word.

Q. Did this man probably perceive what the authority of Christ arose from, — namely, His divine nature, and the divine works that He wrought for a spiritual purpose?

A. Probably not.

Q. What is the meaning of Christ's reply in verse 14?

A. That his office was not to judge and decide questions about property; but to do the far higher work of teaching spiritual truth, and saving men from sin.

Q. What does He then tell those about Him to beware of?

A. Covetousness.

Q. What is "covetousness"?

A. An eager passion for accumulating money or property.

Q. Does it seem from this, that Jesus perceived something of this bad passion in the man who had just spoken to Him?

A. It does.

Q. What do you understand by the expression, "a man's life consisteth not in the abundance of the things which he possesseth"?

A. That our deepest life and true happiness do not depend on the amount of our property, or our luxuries.

Q. What do they depend on?

A. On our faithfulness in doing our duty, and our faith in God.

Q. What, then, is the direct object of this parable?

A. To enforce the truth just stated.

Q. Is it implied that the rich man was guilty of any wrong in acquiring his wealth?

A. It is not; his soil was fruitful (verse 16).

Q. What do you infer from verses 17 and 18?

A. That his crops were so plentiful that he had no place to store them in.

Q. What does he resolve to do?

A. (See verse 18.)

Q. How would the meaning of verse 19 be made more plain?

A. By placing the word "self," instead of the word "soul."

Q. What appears from this verse?

A. That the rich man was thoughtless, empty-minded, and worldly.

Q. What does he propose to do that is unworthy of a man, and an immortal soul?

A. To give himself up to his low appetites, to eating, and drinking, and idleness.

Q. What might you infer from his language to himself?

A. That he expected to live in this world forever.

Q. What terrible warning did he receive which startled him out of this sensual state?

A. God speaks to him, and tells him that on that very night he should die (verse 20).

Q. What is the force of the question at the end of that verse?

A. To show that at the moment of his death his possessions could be his no longer, but he must leave them all behind him.

Q. What must be the rich man's feeling at this announcement?

A. Disappointment, shame, and terror.

Q. How does Jesus give us the lesson of this parable?

A. By saying that all those who selfishly strive to make themselves comfortable, neglecting others, and forgetting God, will be like this miserable man.

Q. What is meant by being "rich toward God"?

A. Those are "rich toward God" who love Him and keep His commandments.

Q. If we do this, need we be afraid when we are told that we must die?

A. We need not, because then we may be sure of being safe and happy with God after we die.

Q. What is the difference, then, between the worldly-minded person and the true Christian, when both come to die?

A. The first will be separated forever from what he loves most, because he loves earthly things most; while the good man, who has found his chief pleasure in duty, faith, and love, will carry these with him, in his soul, into the other world.

Q. What is the only thing that makes dying really fearful?

A. Sin; but if we are Christ's, we can look forward to death calmly and cheerfully.

Q. Might not this rich man have kept himself from becoming so much bound up in his riches and luxury?

A. He might if he had chosen; he might have been a good man, and lived virtuously and died peacefully.

Q. If we find ourselves becoming selfish, how can we resist that tendency?

A. By taking pains to make sacrifices for the sake of others, and by devoting ourselves to rendering them happy. (See v. 33.)

Q. If we do this, what may we hope for?

A. God will look upon us with favor and bless us; for He loves those that love their fellow-creatures.

Q. What other passage teaches us the same solemn lesson with this parable?

A. St. Matt. xvi. 26.

Q. What is the main object of the beautiful words of Jesus that follow this parable, — through verse 31?

A. He continues to compare anxiety for earthly things with the nobler anxiety to be pure and holy.

Q. What does He say respecting anxiety for earthly things?

A. That we should do all our duty, and then leave the result entirely to our Heavenly Father.

Q. But while we are comparatively indifferent to worldly possessions, what does He say we should seek, earnestly and continually?

A. " The kingdom of God"; that is, to obey the precepts of the gospel, follow our Saviour in holiness of life, and help build up and extend His Church; and then we may hope to enter, when we die, into the glory and joy of heaven.

Q. Why does Jesus call this man a "fool"?

A. Because he was willing to lose an eternity of holy and blessed life for the sake of being rich.

Q. The rich man says "*my* goods"; is what we call our property really ours?

A. It is God's more than ours; He only lends it to us; and unless we use it, and give it, for Him and His Church, we have no right at all to it.

Q. What is the least part of our money that we should give for Christ?

A. One tenth. (Lev. xxvii. 32; Gen. xxviii. 22.)

LESSON XVIII.

PARABLE OF THE MASTER AND HIS SERVANTS.

Q. What parable follows immediately after that of the man with many goods?

A. That of the master and his servants.

Q. In what respect does this resemble the preceding?

A. In showing how we are to be truly prepared for change and death.

Q. What is the extent of the whole passage, including this parable?

A. St. Luke xii., from verse 35 to verse 48.

Q. Whom is each one of us compared to in this par-

A. To a servant whose master is absent from home at a wedding.

Q. How ought such a servant to conduct?

A. He ought to "watch" for his master's return, and be ready to receive him, and wait upon him the moment he arrives (verses 35–38).

Q. What is meant by the phrase "having the loins girded"?

A. It is an allusion to a custom of the East, where servants who wait at table wear long robes drawn up, or *girded* up, about their persons.

Q. If a servant were thus clothed, and had his lamps lighted or "burning," what would he be ready to do when his master should arrive?

A. To open the door and do his master's bidding.

Q. What are the *watches* mentioned in verse 38?

A. The night was divided, when this was said, into four watches, of three hours each, — the first commencing at six o'clock in the evening, the second at nine o'clock in the evening, the third at midnight, and the fourth at three o'clock in the morning.

Q. If the master arrived, then, in the "second watch," or the "third watch," at what time would he arrive?

A. If in the "second watch," between nine o'clock and midnight; if in the third, between midnight and three o'clock.

Q. What is the design of verse 39?

A. To show the need of being always watchful and prepared, that we may be guarded against evil as against a thief.

Q. What is probably signified by that "coming of the Son of Man," which Jesus tells His followers to be always ready for?

A. His reappearance on the earth.

Q. If He thought it important for His followers to be seriously *ready* for *that* trial, is it not at least equally important for each one of us to be prepared for the solemn hour of death?

A. This is certainly one application we are to make of His words.

Q. How is it true that this and other great changes come at an *hour when we think not?*

A. They are generally sudden, — not fully foreseen.

Q. What does the Saviour describe in verses 42–44?

A. The character of the good servant, who *does* watch and wait for his master's arrival.

Q. What does He say is the reward of such a servant?

A. That he is promoted to the office of steward, and intrusted with the care of all the household.

Q. How is the wicked and unfaithful servant said to conduct?

A. To indulge in all sorts of violence, wastefulness, and excess, because his master is out of sight (verse 45).

Q. What is the fearful end of such a servant?

A. (See verse 46.)

Q. Who of us are like this wicked servant, and must expect to share in his misery and shame?

A. Those who are careless about their duty, and who do not make earnest efforts to lead Christian lives.

Q. What is the import of verses 47 and 48?

A. That just in proportion as we *know* what is right, we are under solemn obligations to *do* what is right, and that we are and always shall be judged according to the gifts, knowledge, helps, and opportunities that we have.

Q. Does not this require us, who have so many religious opportunities and privileges, to lead very holy lives?

A. It does, and we should never be satisfied with ourselves, as God can never be satisfied with us, unless we improve our many advantages.

Q. What are some of these advantages that we enjoy?

A. We live where we are instructed in the Faith of Jesus Christ; we have friends who show us how we ought to live; and we have before us many excellent examples that we may imitate.

Q. What, now, is the great lesson you may derive from this parable?

A. That it is my duty to be prepared for every change of condition, and especially for the last change, death.

Q. How are you to be prepared for it?

A. By actively and cheerfully serving Christ.

Q. How will this prepare you for death?

A. It will make me sure of His approbation and His support; and if I have this I am prepared for any thing.

Q. Can death be really terrible to those that follow Christ?

A. It cannot, for in Christ they have eternal life, and He will be their Friend after death.

Q. Provided you love your fellow-men and your Saviour, how may you meet death?

A. Calmly and happily, for I know that *then* death cannot harm me.

LESSON XIX.

PARABLE OF THE BARREN FIG-TREE.

Q. WHICH of the four Evangelists gives an account of this parable, and where?
A. St. Luke, in chap. xiii., verses 6–9.
Q. How do we learn what called it forth?
A. By looking at the preceding verses of the chapter.
Q. What did some persons remind Jesus of at this time?
A. Of Pilate's commanding some Galileans to be put to death by the sword, at the very moment when they were offering sacrifices in the Temple, so that their blood flowed down, and was "mingled with their sacrifices."
Q. Who was Pilate?
A. He was a cruel and obstinate man, at that time governor of Judea, being sent from Rome by the Roman government to fill that office. (See St. Matt. xxvii. 2.)
Q. Why should the governor of Judea be sent from Rome?
A. Because Judea was then a province governed by the Roman empire.
Q. What did Jesus say to those who reminded Him of Pilate's killing those Galileans?
A. He said that many other Galileans really deserved such punishment as much as those who suffered it (verse 2).
Q. What other case of the destruction of human life does Jesus mention?
A. Of the falling of a tower, built probably over the pool of Siloam at Jerusalem (St. John ix. 7), which crushed eighteen persons.

Q. What does He say, in verses 3 and 5, with reference to those that perished in these ways?

A. That among those who heard Him speak were many, who, unless they repented of their sins, must perish as miserably.

Q. Whom did He especially warn by these words?

A. The Jewish nation.

Q. What made the Jewish nation at that time so deserving of severe punishments?

A. They had grown corrupt, sinful in their lives, and hypocritical in their religion; and because the Saviour preached righteousness to them, and reproved their sins, they soon after put Him to death on the cross.

Q. Having thus uttered a solemn warning to this people, Jesus enforces it by a parable; will you read or repeat that parable?

Q. Whom does the man that planted the fig-tree in the vineyard represent, in the parable?

A. God, who plants the nations on earth.

Q. What particular nation is intended by this fig-tree?

A. The Jews.

Q. What was the great sin of the Jews?

A. As the tree bore no fruit in figs, so they did not bear fruit in righteous actions.

Q. Who may be meant by the "dresser," or gardener, of the vineyard?

A. His Son, our Saviour.

Q. What does the owner of the vineyard say to the dresser?

A. (Verse 7.)

Q. What do you understand by the expression "Why cumbereth it the ground?"

A. "Why should this tree, which bears no fruit, be allowed to stand here and *cumber*, or *occupy uselessly*, the ground, when a fruitful tree might be planted in its place."

Q. Will you put the meaning of this into other language, as it would be applied to the Jewish nation?

A. "Why should this nation, which, after all the religious privileges they have enjoyed, continue selfish and proud, be allowed to stand in their power, setting a bad example before others, and thus cumbering the earth."

Q. What is the "dresser" represented as urging, in behalf of this people, in verses 8 and 9?

A. As pleading that they may be spared from destruction yet a little longer, that some new efforts may be made to awaken them to their duty, and make them repent and be saved.

Q. What did the Saviour do in His "this year also"?

A. He suffered on the cross, — His mightiest act of mercy.

Q. What do we learn from history respecting the fulfillment of these warnings to the Jews?

A. A few years after they were indeed "cut down"; the Roman armies came and completely destroyed their chief city, Jerusalem, and butchered men, women, and children; so that they actually perished very much like those whom Pilate killed, and those on whom the tower of Siloam fell.

Q. Has not this parable an application to us also?

A. It has; for God's law is over us, as well as over the Jews.

Q. What does it teach you?

A. That unless I improve my opportunities, and grow in goodness, I must look for a terrible judgment from my God.

Q. What is your great opportunity ?

A. That of continually learning more of my Saviour, and gaining more of His Spirit.

Q. What is your great privilege ?

A. That of having religious instruction, knowing the teachings and life of Christ, and receiving the ordinances of the Church.

Q. If, then, you do not grow better, but cling to your sinful ways and low passions, what are you ?

A. But a cumberer of the ground, unworthy to fill my place here, which God intended for His good children.

Q. What, then, ought to be your resolution to-day ?

A. That I will sincerely repent of all the evil I have done, and be changed into a truly obedient and loving child of God.

Q. If you do this what has your Heavenly Father promised ?

A. That I shall have peace in my soul, and that He will bless me in this life and the life to come.

Q. The vine-dresser interceded or pleaded for the barren tree ; what are we told of Christ's intercession for us ?

A. (Heb. vii. 25 ; 1 John ii. 1, 2.)

LESSON XX.

THE PARABLE OF THE GREAT SUPPER.

Q. Where do you find the parable of the great supper?

A. In St. Luke xiv. 16 to 25.

LESSONS ON THE PARABLES. 87

Q. Will you read carefully this chapter xiv., from verse 1 up to verse 16, where the parable begins?

Q. On what occasion was the parable spoken?

A. It appears from verse 1 that Jesus was "eating bread," that is he was *dining*, at the house of a distinguished Jew.

Q. Did the Jews make more than common preparations for dinner on the Sabbath?

A. They did, for they thought that they honored the day, and showed their respect for their religion by spreading a sumptuous feast.

Q. Was their Sabbath like our Sabbath?

A. Not in many respects; for while it was a day of feasting with them, with us it is a day of worship and spiritual improvement.

Q. Should we think it right to take up our time, or the time of our family domestics, with providing a more expensive and luxurious dinner on Sunday than on other days?

A. We should not; for then both we and they would have less time to attend worship, and read good books, and visit the sick and poor.

Q. Would not the luxurious dinner be apt to tempt us to excessive eating?

A. It would, and in that way make us stupid and dull, and less inclined to give our minds freely to religious instruction.

Q. What was the direction that Jesus proceeded to give to those about him?

A. (Read verses 8-10; also St. Matt. xxiii. 6.)

Q. What is the general application of this passage that we ought to make?

A. We should learn to be humble; not to put ourselves forward immodestly in any thing; to give others the best place, and more respect and more credit than we give ourselves.

Q. What does Christ mean when He says that humble persons shall "have worship" (verse 10)?

A. He means that others will honor and love them, because they are humble.

Q. Will you read verses 12–14?

Q. Does Jesus mean to say, in verse 12, that we really ought not to invite our friends, and relatives, and rich neighbors to our houses at all?

A. Not by any means. He teaches that it will be a mean motive if we invite them *for the sake of being invited by them in return.*

Q. What else do we learn from these three verses?

A. That it is much more noble, and much more acceptable to God, for us to feed the poor, and to be kind to the unfortunate, the lowly, and the sick, than to make a display of entertainments and parties of pleasure for the rich and comfortable, to gratify our pride.

Q. To whom were these three verses peculiarly addressed by Jesus?

A. To those who *make* entertainments, as the previous verses had been addressed to those who *attend* them.

Q. What did the man probably mean by "eats bread in the kingdom of God"?

A. He was probably thinking only of his superiority as a Jew, not as a Christian.

Q. How does it appear that sharing in the peace and wisdom of Christian faith may be compared to "eating bread"?

A. That faith, and the truth of Christ, nourish the soul's life, as bread nourishes the body. (See St. John vi. 32–35.)

Q. What reply does Jesus make to this person's remark?

A. He replies by this parable of the Great Supper. (The pupil may repeat or read it.)

Q. How do you explain it, that in all these several passages Jesus makes constant allusions to feasts or suppers?

A. It was His custom to take His subject from some passing event, or present object; and at this moment He was at a feast, which suggested to Him His language.

Q. In verse 16, are we to suppose that those persons whom the man sent his servant to call in to his supper had been previously invited?

A. We are; and that they had accepted the invitation, or promised to come.

Q. How are we to regard their conduct, then, in offering the excuses which are written in verses 18–20 for staying away?

A. They broke their promises, and were guilty of great incivility to the individual who had kindly invited them.

Q. How did that individual feel under such treatment?

A. He felt a natural indignation.

Q. Does the word "anger" or "angry" (verse 21), as used in the Bible, always refer to that anger which is wicked?

A. It does not; it sometimes signifies an indignation at injustice, or meanness, or sin, which is not wrong. (See Eph. iv. 26, and all those passages in the Old Testament where God is said to be angry; as Psalm vii. 11, and Numbers xxv. 3.)

Q. What is that wicked anger which degrades us and displeases God?

A. It is the passion that makes us wish to do some harm to others, and takes away our self-control.

Q. Will you refer to some passages in the Bible which show us that such anger is very wrong?

A. Prov. xiv. 17, xvi. 32; Eccles. vii. 9; St. Matt. v. 22; Eph. iv. 31.

Q. What other reasons have we for knowing that angry passions are wrong?

A. Our conscience tells us so, and we feel ashamed and uncomfortable after we have indulged them.

Q. What did the master of the house tell his servant to do, after his invitations had been so slighted?

A. To go out and call in to his supper "the poor," "the maimed" or crippled, "the halt" or lame, and "the blind."

Q. In order that all the room might be filled, he sent out a second time; what did he mean by telling the servant to "*compel* them to come in"?

A. He wished to have them urgently entreated — even those poor beggars that sit by the highways and hedges — to come.

Q. Was it customary for some of the Jews to provide entertainments for poor people?

A. It was.

Q. Turn now to the spiritual lesson of the parable; and whom may we consider to be intended by the "master of the house" who gave the supper?

A. Our Father in heaven.

Q. What is the "supper" He provides?

A. The spiritual feast of the gospel in the Church.

Q. Who is the "servant," or messenger, that comes to call men to this supper?

A. Jesus Christ, calling by His ministers.

Q. Who are meant by those persons that were first "bidden," or invited?

A. The Jews; because Christ appeared and lived among them in Judea; and thus His gospel or teaching, which is "the supper," was first offered to them.

Q. How did they refuse to accept the offer?

A. By not believing what Christ said, but persecuting and scorning Him, and at last putting Him to death.

Q. Who are signified by those "poor," "maimed," "halt," and "blind"?

A. The people, not Jews, but belonging to other nations, called Gentiles.

Q. Why were these represented as being such poor outcasts?

A. Because up to the time when Christ lived they had not enjoyed so many advantages of instruction and help as the Jews had for knowing the truth.

Q. When the Apostles went abroad soon after, however, and preached the gospel to them, did they gladly receive it?

A. They did; so that the parable proved true, and these poor Gentiles enjoyed the "supper" of the holy instructions of Christ, while the Jews shut themselves out by their unbelieving and selfish dispositions.

Q. What should we learn by this?

A. That the poor, ignorant, and weak, if they try, may be good and happy, and go to heaven, as well as the rich, and the fashionable, and the well-dressed children. (1 Cor. i. 26–29.)

Q. What may *you* learn from what is said of excuses in this parable?

A. That I cannot have any *good* excuse for not doing right; and that if I love my earthly pleasure or possessions more than my duty and my Saviour, I am in danger of losing my own soul.

LESSON XXI.

PARABLES OF THE TOWER, AND OF THE KING GOING TO WAR.

Q. Where do you find these parables concerning the tower, and the king going to war?

A. They follow directly after the parable of the last lesson, in the 14th chapter of St. Luke's Gospel.

Q. What are we told in verse 25?

A. That multitudes of people went with Him.

Q. Why did they follow Him?

A. They were drawn around Him by the striking truths He uttered, by the simplicity and beauty of His life, and by His miraculous works.

Q. What may we naturally suppose respecting the voice and appearance of Jesus?

A. That a person so full of goodness and love must have been wonderfully attractive, and that He spoke with tones of earnestness and sincerity.

Q. What seems to have been Christ's object in what He immediately said to these multitudes that were following Him (verse 26)?

A. To show them that if they really intended to become His followers, they must not expect to find it an easy thing, but a work of great difficulty and self-denial.

Q. What do you understand by being a follower of Jesus Christ?

A. Believing on Him, acting from that spirit of goodness and love that He always displayed, and trying to live like Him.

Q. Ought we to consider this an easy task?

A. It cannot be easy; it must cost us exertion.

Q. But shall we be afraid of that exertion?

A. Never, for He will be our friend, and will give us a noble reward.

Q. What will that reward be?

A. An approving conscience, a peaceful heart, and eternal joy in heaven.

Q. Does Jesus mean, in verse 26, that we must *absolutely hate* our father and mother and other relatives, in order to be His followers?

A. He cannot mean this; for He teaches us, in all parts of His instructions, to *love* all mankind, to love our kindred and acquaintances, — not to hate them.

Q. How does it happen that this word "hate" is used here?

A. Jesus spoke in the Greek language, and the words that He used did not convey to those who heard Him any such meaning as " hate "; but the men who translated the New Testament from the Greek into our English language placed this word here.

Q. How might they have expressed Christ's meaning more accurately?

A. By writing thus: "If any man come to me, he cannot be truly my disciple, unless he loves me more than he loves his father, or mother, or wife, or children, or brethren, or sisters, or his own life."

Q. Is not this shown to be exactly what Christ did say, in St. Matthew's Gospel?

A. It is. (See St. Matt. x. 37.)

Q. What then do you understand by this saying of Christ?

A. That I must love all my earthly friends less than I love my Friend and Saviour, Christ; and that I must obey my conscience and my Maker, even if I should be obliged, in doing so, to displease some companion or relative.

Q. What does Jesus go on to say in verse 27, and what does He mean by telling us we must "bear the cross"?

A. Those who believed on Christ and followed Him were persecuted by the Jews, who did not wish to believe Him, on account of their prejudices and sins; and as these unbelievers were the strongest party, they sometimes cruelly put the followers of Christ to death, by stretching them on two pieces of wood nailed together in the form of a *cross.* This was a common form of capital punishment.

Q. Where is the account of Christ's own death on such a cross, that is, His crucifixion?

A. In St. Luke, chapter xxiii.; St. Mark, chapter xv.; St. Matthew, chapter xxvii.; St. John, chapter xix.

Q. Why does Jesus speak of these awful dangers beforehand?

A. He is always open and candid; He wishes these people to understand that they will have to meet such trials; and He warns them that unless they are ready to endure them they cannot be His disciples.

Q. Suppose that a person should forsake the path of duty, and do wrong, through his fear of others, what kind of a character would he have?

A. A mean and cowardly character.

Q. Will you state now the meaning of the parable of "building the tower," verses 28–30?

A. Jesus shows us that before making up our minds

to be Christians we must "count the cost"; that is, look at the difficulties and trials it will cost us; just as a man counts the cost of a tower before he begins to build it.

Q. What kind of a "tower" is referred to here?

A. In that country, the tops of the houses were flat, so that persons could walk about on them; a *tower* was built up on the roof, and contained some small rooms for places of retirement and prayer. Sometimes towers were built in the fields for the use of farmers, and sometimes on city walls for observations in war. Probably this was a tower in the field.

Q. What other illustration does Jesus give of the importance of counting the cost of an undertaking beforehand?

A. (See verses 32 and 33.)

Q. How does Jesus sum up the lesson of this passage in verse 33?

A. That if we are not ready to forsake every thing else for His sake, we are not fit to be His disciples.

Q. What was the chief reason that He and His first followers were obliged to suffer so much for their faith?

A. It was because His gospel was so much opposed to the wickedness and errors of mankind. They persecuted Him because He reproved their sins.

Q. What is the great trial that *we* are called to undergo in being Christians?

A. We are obliged to deny ourselves all sinful pleasures, and sometimes to be ridiculed and despised.

Q. From what quarter do most of our temptations come?

A. From our own self-love and sensual passions.

Q. What then should we pray that we may become?

A. More and more spiritually-minded.

Q. Will you mention, in your own words, some of the ways in which you think you are most likely to do wrong?

Q. How should you act if other persons blame you, or ridicule you, for doing what is right?

A. I should be above it, and persevere in my duty.

Q. What glorious promise does Jesus make to those who take this Christian course?

A. (See St. Matt. xix. 29.)

LESSON XXII.

PARABLE OF THE LOST SHEEP, AND OF THE LOST PIECE OF SILVER.

Q. WHAT drew from Christ the parables recorded in the fifteenth chapter of St. Luke's Gospel?

A. The fact (v. 1) that, as Jesus was teaching, the "publicans and sinners" came near to hear His instructions.

Q. Who were the "publicans" mentioned here?

A. They were men who had it for their business to collect taxes from the Jewish people, to be paid over to the government.

Q. What made their character and office especially odious and unpopular?

A. The fact that these taxes which they collected, and which the people were obliged to pay, were levied by the Emperor of Rome, a foreign ruler, and went to the Roman empire. Besides, for a Jew thus to serve the foreign government, was considered disloyal.

LESSONS ON THE PARABLES. 97

Q. How did it happen that the Jews were obliged to pay taxes to the Roman government?

A. The armies of that government had at this time conquered Judea, and held it in subjection.

Q. What further made the publican contemptible?

A. He sometimes went beyond the authority given him, and exacted from the people larger sums than were due.

Q. How do we find publicans spoken of frequently in the New Testament?

A. In connection with sinners, as if they were despised. St. Luke v. 30.

Q. Did Jesus despise them?

A. He never despised any human soul; although He rebuked all their sins, He pitied their condition, and longed to save them.

Q. Who were the " Pharisees and Scribes " mentioned in verse 2?

A. They were classes of men very strict in performing such outward actions as their law enjoined upon them, and who spent much time in studying that law and disputing about it.

Q. What was their character generally?

A. They were cold-hearted and selfish, more careful to perform particular ceremonies than to cherish in their hearts those good affections, or to do those benevolent deeds, which Christ loved.

Q. Where do you find how Christ regarded them, and their outside formality, separated from holiness and love?

A. In St. Matt. v. 20, in a large part of chap. xxiii., and St. Luke xx. 46.

Q. What does he plainly imply respecting them in many places?

7

A. That though they pretended to despise publicans and sinners, and refused to go near them, yet they themselves had as many faults; such as pride, self-righteousness, insincerity, love of the world, and uncharitableness.

Q. What may we learn from this?

A. Not to be forward to accuse others of doing wrong while our own characters are open to rebuke.

Q. Suppose we have not those sins which some others have, what becomes us still?

A. To consider whether we are not guilty of some other sins which, though different, are just as bad.

Q. To show His reason for being in the company of sinners, Jesus proceeds to deliver a parable in verses 3–6; will you repeat this parable of the lost sheep?

Q. What is the amount of this parable?

A. That if a man have a flock of a hundred sheep, and lose one of them, he will leave the remaining ninety-nine to take care of themselves, while he searches for the lost one; and if he finds it, he feels a more lively pleasure in it than in the fact that the other ninety-nine have stayed in their places, and have not been lost.

Q. What, now, is the application Christ would make of this parable?

A. He would compare the sinner — the bad man — to that lost sheep, and Himself to the shepherd who goes out to seek for him, to bring him back to goodness and eternal life.

Q. Will you explain how it should ever happen that one of a flock of sheep should be lost in that country?

A. Many of the men of Judea kept sheep as their occupation, and as they did not confine them to any one pasture, but drove them from place to place in various directions, as the seasons changed, it was not strange that, in some wild place or "wilderness," a single sheep should wander away from the rest.

Q. Using this comparison of the parable, if the sinful man, or the sinful child, is the "lost sheep," who is the good shepherd that seeks for him to bring him back to the fold?

A. Jesus, the Saviour, who came into the world to bring wandering sinners home to Himself, and home to heaven.

Q. In what other passages is Christ represented as the "Good Shepherd" of the sheep?

A. In several verses of St. John x., in Heb. xiii. 20, and 1 Pet. ii. 25, and v. 4.

Q. If, then, Christ is the Shepherd, what is His fold?

A. As the sheepfold is the place where the sheep gather to rest at night, so the fold of those who follow Christ is in the society of His disciples, — the Church.

Q. How does this Divine Shepherd save the "lost sheep"?

A. Is. liii. 6; St. John x. 11.

Q. How are the "Pharisees" contrasted with the Good Shepherd?

A. (See Ezekiel xxxiv. 8–11.)

Q. How does Jesus illustrate the truth conveyed by this parable in another form?

A. By a very similar parable in verses 8 and 9, in which he asks if a woman would not feel a keener joy in finding *one* piece of silver that she had lost, than in keeping *nine* safely in her possession.

Q. The Saviour concludes both of these parables in nearly the same words (see verses 7 and 10); what is the meaning of verse 10?

A. That those happy and pure spirits which are ever

with God, feel a holy joy whenever any one of us repents and returns to Him.

Q. What do you understand by verse 7?

A. That there is a more *vivid* and *intense* satisfaction felt at such an unexpected change in a bad person's character, than in the regular course of those who have not been in the sinner's danger and misery.

Q. What other explanation can be offered?

A. That Christ meant that there is more joy in heaven over one sinner that repenteth, than over ninety and nine persons like the scribes and Pharisees, who *think themselves* just, who think they have no need of repentance, and therefore do not repent.

Q. Why, then, did the Saviour go among publicans and sinners?

A. (Ezekiel xxxiv. 12–16.)

Q. If, then, God our Saviour so loves mankind and wants to deliver them from the misery of sinful habits and bad passions, how ought we to regard all vicious persons, inebriates, and criminals?

A. With great compassion, because they are under this awful darkness of sin, and need our pity.

Q. If sinful persons seem happy, do they need our compassion the less?

A. Not at all, for sooner or later their sin will make them wretched.

Q. While we pity and love the person that commits sin, as Jesus did, on account of his immortal soul and the injury he inflicts upon it, how should we regard sin itself?

A. We should despise it, and resist it, and shun it, whether in our own breasts or elsewhere.

Q. When we see how Jesus answered the proud " scribes

and Pharisees," who thought it *beneath* them to notice " publicans and sinners," — showing that even He, who was so much higher and purer than they, did not think it beneath Him, — what should we learn from it?

A. Not to think of ourselves more highly than we think of others, but to remember that we also are sinners.

Q. What should occur to us when we see vicious and criminal persons?

A. That, if it were not for our friends and the circumstances of our education, we too might have been as bad as they.

Q. What feeling should this awaken?

A. Gratitude for the mercy that we have been kept from being worse than we are.

Q. And what resolution should it inspire us with?

A. To strive, that, as our condition is more favorable than that of many others, we are called upon in the sight of God to have better characters than they, and to grow rapidly and steadily into Christ.

LESSON XXIII.

PARABLE OF THE PRODIGAL SON.

Q. WHAT seems to have been the occasion of Christ's delivering the parable of the prodigal son?

A. He delivered it immediately after those two that we examined in the preceding lesson; and it seems to have been called out by the same cause, namely, the complaint of the Pharisees that he mingled with publicans and sinners. St. Luke xv. 11.

Q. What does Jesus show us by this parable?

A. That whenever the sinful forsake their wicked ways, and come in penitent prayer to their Heavenly Father, asking forgiveness, He will forgive them, and restore them.

Q. If we study the parable closely, what else shall we find?

A. That the story describes, figuratively, the whole course of a young man, through temptation, sin, repentance, and conversion.

Q. Jesus begins with imagining a father as having two sons; what does the younger of these sons ask?

A. He asks his father to give him his part of the property, whatever it may be, at once, instead of waiting for his father to give it to him when he should see fit; and this was his first misstep.

Q. Why was this wrong?

A. It showed an unbecoming haste in the young man to get possession of the property, and also a bad desire to escape from the control of his father, for the sake of following his own will.

Q. Did the father comply with this request of his son?

A. He did, for he probably saw that his heart was estranged and would not be satisfied till he had tried his own way.

Q. What foolish course did the young man take next?

A. He collected all his money, travelled into a far off place, and there wasted it all in idleness and dissipation (verse 13).

Q. What better way can you point out, that he might have followed?

A. He might have devoted himself industriously, temperately, and happily to some useful business.

Q. We are then told (v. 14) that, after all his money was spent, his distress was made more severe by a great famine that arose in the land where he was; what is a famine?

A. A scarcity of food, arising generally from an unfruitful season, and making provisions very costly; this would increase the young man's distress, as he would find it more difficult to subsist on charity.

Q. In this wretched condition, which he had so foolishly brought upon himself, what did he do?

A. He first, instead of going straight home, turned to other helps. He found employment as a hired laborer for a citizen of that country, and his work was to take care of swine and feed them.

Q. What proof is given us that he was exceedingly poor?

A. He would have been glad to fill himself even with the husks eaten by the swine.

Q. What were these " husks"?

A. They were pods which grew on the carob tree, — a coarse article of food.

Q. Does not every young man who becomes dissipated and sensual plunge himself into as great misery as this, whether he wanders to a distance from home or not?

A. He does, because his worst destitution and suffering is always in his conscience and his heart. If we will not freely be God's servants, we must be the world's slaves.

Q. In verse 17, it is said that this prodigal young man, when he *came to himself*, contrasted his miserable condition with that of even the servants in the distant home of his father; what is the peculiar force of this phrase " he came to himself"?

A. During his vicious and thoughtless course thus far, he had been like one *beside himself*, morally deranged; and when he began to reflect seriously, and to remember that beautiful home that he had forsaken, and to long to return, it was *coming to himself;* it was coming to his right senses again.

Q. What right resolution did the young man take then?

A. (Verse 18.)

Q. What is especially impressive in this good resolution?

A. That he was determined to confess his faults; not to pretend proudly that he had done right, but to say, as he felt, " Father, I have sinned against Heaven and before thee."

Q. What other beautiful trait does he show?

A. He does not *claim* his father's compassion, for he feels that he does not deserve it; but he very humbly trusts to the forgiving love of his father to give him the lowly place of a servant.

Q. Did he put his good resolution into practice?

A. He did (v. 20); and this is the only way in which our purposes can have any value; if we do not *act* upon them, they are good for nothing.

Q. How did his father feel toward him and receive him?

A. With all a father's tender affection and joy to see him return once more.

Q. When the young man uttered his sorrowful confession (v. 21), what did the father reply?

A. He gave such a reply as showed his gladness, and how ready he was to forgive all his son's bad conduct; and he gave directions to have those things done which were customary in that country, and were the tokens of the utmost rejoicing.

Q. In reading the remainder of the chapter, you perceive that the elder son, who had remained all this time at home with his father, felt angry when he found so much pleasure was excited by his wicked brother's return; what seems to have been precisely his feeling?

A. Jealousy that his father gave so much attention to his younger brother.

Q. What ought he to have remembered?

A. That all this time this younger brother had been suffering the dreadful consequences of his dissolute and vicious life, while he, the elder, had been enjoying the comforts of a regular and obedient life with his father.

Q. What, then, should he have felt?

A. He should have pitied that brother, and have been willing that one who had endured so much for his wickedness should now be encouraged and welcomed back with joy.

Q. Having thus seen how much instruction this parable of the prodigal son gives to all young persons, simply by its plain and literal meaning, what does it teach as an allegory, — *as a parable?*

A. It teaches us not only our duties to our earthly parents, but also respecting our relations to God.

Q. Whom does the *father* of the two sons signify in the parable?

A. Our Father in Heaven, the Father of all mankind.

Q. Who are represented by the two sons?

A. All the children of his human family, — the obedient by the elder son, the disobedient by the younger.

Q. When do all of us wander away from our Heavenly Father's home, like the prodigal who left his father's house?

A. Whenever we set up our own will above the Law of God.

Q. When may we be said to be in the *far-off country?*

A. When we are living for selfish pleasure, without Christian principle, and without prayer.

Q. What is the famine of the spirit?

A. (Amos viii. 11.)

Q. When may we be said, like the prodigal, to *come to ourselves?*

A. When we begin to feel earnestly that we are doing wrong, and long to do better.

Q. What is this feeling?

A. Repentance.

Q. If it is sincere and true repentance, what will it lead us to do?

A. To go to God in prayer, as the prodigal goes in the parable to his father, and humbly entreat Him to forgive us, and look upon us once more with favor, and help us to return.

Q. Can we return without that help?

A. (St. John vi. 44.)

Q. By showing us how the young man's father received his son, what does Jesus teach us respecting our reception by God?

A. He shows us that God will always be ready to answer our prayers and pardon us.

Q. What other sure pledge have we of this truth?

A. Jesus Christ Himself gave up His own life and died on the cross to obtain forgiveness for us.

Q. On this account, in whose name should we offer our prayers when we pray for pardon?

A. In the name of Jesus Christ our Lord. St. John xvi. 23.

Q. How should we feel towards our fellow-creatures who have been very sinful, but are struggling to reform?

A. We should not be jealous of them, as the elder son in the parable was of the younger, but we should rejoice in their conversion.

Q. What more should we be ready to do?

A. To assist them in their good exertions, to encourage them, and to try to make duty delightful to them.

LESSON XXIV.

PARABLE OF THE UNJUST STEWARD.

Q. WHERE do you find the Saviour's parable of the unjust steward?

A. In the first eight verses of the sixteenth chapter of St. Luke's Gospel; the five verses following also contain words of the Saviour that relate to the parable and explain it.

Q. To whom did Jesus address this parable?

A. To His own disciples and friends, for their instruction. (Verse 1.)

Q. To whom had He been addressing the three preceding parables that we have studied, written in the preceding chapter?

A. To the scribes and Pharisees. (Verses 2, 3.)

Q. What is a "steward"?

A. He is an officer, belonging to the household of a

rich man, who acts as an agent in managing the affairs of his employer, and in keeping his accounts.

Q. What was the accusation brought against this steward?

A. Some one informed his employer that the steward had been neglectful, or dishonest, or both, and had thus wasted his master's goods, instead of saving them carefully, as it was his duty to do.

Q. What course did the rich man pursue?

A. He called the steward to him, told him to make a statement of all his transactions, and informed him that he must leave his place on account of his misconduct.

Q. As the steward then deliberates what he shall do for a living, why does he say that he "cannot dig"?

A. Either he was not strong enough in health for such hard labor as digging the earth, or else he did not understand that kind of work.

Q. It seems that he could think of no occupation that would afford him a livelihood; but why could he not "beg"?

A. He felt that shame at becoming a beggar, which is natural to us all.

Q. Why do we feel this shame?

A. Because we know that it is more honorable for us to earn our own support, than it is to ask others to maintain us out of what belongs to themselves.

Q. What was the amount of the resolution he formed, spoken of in verse 4?

A. He resolved to do something to lay those who owed debts to his employer under an obligation to himself.

Q. What was his object in this?

A. To make them feel thankful to him, and thus willing to furnish him a home in their houses.

Q. Will you explain how he proceeded to do this in the first case?

A. He sent for one of those who owed his employer, and told him to take the writing, or note, wherein he had engaged to pay a hundred measures of oil, erase the words, and put down instead only fifty measures of oil. (Verses 5 and 6.)

Q. How did this help the debtor?

A. It reduced his debt one half; so that when the time came for paying the rich man, that debtor was bound by the new writing to pay only half as much as he would have been obliged to pay if the old writing had been kept. For this favor he must thank the steward.

Q. What kind of oil was this that was mentioned here?

A. A sweet oil that was obtained from the fruit of the olive-tree in Palestine.

Q. What was it used for?

A. It was valuable for burning in lamps (see Exodus xxvii. 20); for food, to be eaten like butter (see 1 Kings xvii. 12); and for anointing the body (see St. Luke vii. 46).

Q. How much did one "measure" (or bath) of this oil contain?

A. As many as nine gallons.

Q. What did the steward do to make himself acceptable to another person?

A. He told him to alter his "bill," or contract, in a similar way, so that instead of having to pay a hundred measures of wheat he should only have to pay fourscore measures, that is, eighty.

Q. And how much did a measure of wheat contain?

A. About eleven bushels.

Q. Does it appear that the steward defrauded his employer of these sums by reducing the amount of the debts in this way?

A. Not of course. He may have intended to make up the deficiency himself, and to pay over to his employer, out of his own income, as much as these debtors were excused from paying.

Q. How is it probable these debts were incurred?

A. They were, we may presume, a portion of the produce of land hired by these men as tenants of "the rich man," and were due to him as rent.

Q. Why is the rich man called "lord" in the 5th and 8th verses?

A. The word "lord" means here "master," or "owner of the land," and "head of the household."

Q. In what light did the rich man regard the character of this steward?

A. He regarded him as *unjust*. (See verses 2 and 8.)

Q. Why did he regard him so?

A. Because he had wasted goods that did not belong to him, and so abused his office, and been unfaithful to his trust; possibly, also, for fraud.

Q. Why did the rich man "commend" his steward then, as it is said he did, in verse 8?

A. He commended him, not for his injustice or prodigality; on that part of his conduct he looked with disapprobation; but he praised him for his prudence, his foresight, in taking so sure a method of making friends and securing a future support from those friends.

Q. How would that support be likely to be given to the steward?

A. These persons that had been favored by the steward would provide for him after he was turned out of his stewardship.

Q. In this respect, how are we to regard his conduct?

A. As merely a shrewd piece of worldly calculation.

Q. Where does the parable properly end?

A. At the word " wisely," in verse 8.

Q. Christ, having concluded the parable, adds these words : " For the children of this world are in their generation wiser than the children of light." Whom does He mean by " the children of this world "?

A. He means those persons who are worldly-minded, — who care for worldly convenience and prosperity, eating and drinking, riches and pleasure, dress and admiration, more than for goodness, and God.

Q. Whom does He mean by " the children of light"?

A. He means the good, who act from Christian principle ; and who, on this account, have their minds and hearts full of peace, clearness, and " light." (See Eph. v. 8 ; 2 Cor. iv. 6.)

Q. What does He mean, then, by saying that the children of this world are, *in their generation,* wiser than the children of light?

A. He means that they are wiser *in worldly things ;* that is, that they often take more pains, and show more careful forethought in gaining earthly good, than Christians do in gaining spiritual and immortal good, wisdom and holiness.

Q. Will you repeat what Christ says, in further explanation of this parable, in verse 9 ?

Q. What do you understand by " the mammon of unrighteousness "?

A. Earthly riches; the perishable things that we possess in this world. (Prov. xxiii. 5; 1 Tim. vi. 17.

Q. How are we to make these our "friends"?

A. Not by becoming too much attached to them, but by so using them that they may strengthen our souls, serve the Church, and increase our disposition to do good. (St. Luke xii. 33.)

Q. In what ways can we thus use them?

A. By avoiding all excess in eating, drinking, dress, and amusement; and by giving a portion of our money to the poor, to feed the hungry, and clothe the destitute, and instruct the ignorant, and send the gospel where it is not known. (St. Mat. xxv. 34–40.)

Q. If we use what property we have in this way, how will it appear as our "friend"?

A. It will be one means of ripening our souls for heaven; and, when we grow old and die, it will have helped prepare us for those "everlasting habitations," where we shall be happy with our Heavenly Father, and Jesus Christ, and all pure sprits, forever.

Q. What does Christ teach in verse 10?

A. That those who act from Christian principle will be as careful to do right in small things as in great; and, on the other hand, that those who are unjust or sinful in any little every-day action, will be likely to do wrong in greater matters.

Q. What, then, is the only safe way?

A. To aim and strive to do right in every thing.

Q. What is the purport of verse 11?

A. Jesus implies that those who are not faithful and honest in their dealings with earthly property, cannot receive the "true riches" of heavenly faith, peace, hope, and eternal life.

Q. How are we to understand verse 12?

A. Whatever we possess on earth belongs not so much to us as to God, who lends us all things. If we do not remember this, and devote all that we have to Him as His servants, but live selfishly, then "our own" peace and heavenly joy will be denied to us.

Q. Are the words "another *man's*" a correct translation from the original?

A. They are not; we should read "that which is another's," referring to the gifts of God.

Q. Will you state the meaning of Jesus in verse 13?

A. That we can have but one ruling desire, one supreme purpose, one "master" of our hearts; that if we try to have two, we shall still love one much more than the other; and that if we would love and serve God heartily, we must be willing to let mammon, or the good things of the earth, go, and deny ourselves, and be content with doing His will, as honor and happiness enough.

Q. Will you state now the application of these truths to the parable of the unjust steward?

A. We are to be careful so to use our present life that we may gain the life everlasting, as the steward used his means to gain a home in the habitations of his friends. (1 St. Peter iv. 10.)

Q. Are we not under much higher motives than he was?

A. Infinitely higher; inasmuch as spiritual riches are more precious than worldly goods, and eternity is longer than our mortal life.

Q. What, then, is the great lesson of this parable?

A. That we are to seek with far more diligence, all

our lives, to be Christ's faithful disciples, than to be comfortable or rich.

LESSON XXV.

PARABLE OF THE RICH MAN AND LAZARUS.

Q. WHAT light may we gain from the connection respecting the parable of the rich man and Lazarus, recorded in St. Luke's Gospel, xvi. 19–31 ?

A. This is one of several parables which seem to have been spoken nearly at the same time; and what first led Jesus to deliver them was the blame thrown upon him by the scribes and Pharisees, because he was kind to publicans and sinners. (St. Luke xv. 1, 2.)

Q. What, then, did he probably wish to teach at this time?

A. That these scribes and Pharisees, and other Jews, proud as they were, had really no better claim to the blessings promised in the gospel than other people, like the Gentiles.

Q. While this was one truth, what other point did he desire now to insist upon, as appears from the lesson preceding this, and from verse 14 of this chapter?

A. That the love of money is a hateful passion, and that they who indulge it bring on themselves misery hereafter.

Q. What other name is sometimes applied to this parable?

A. It is sometimes called the parable of *Dives* and

Lazarus, because *Dives* is the Latin word signifying *rich man*.

Q. What is the meaning of the name *Lazarus* in the original?

A. It is the same as "Eleazar," and means "one who is helped by God."

Q. How is the poverty of Lazarus touchingly represented in contrast with this great wealth of Dives?

A. (See verses 20 and 21.) Only "crumbs" were asked for.

Q. Was it customary in those days for the poor to receive food in charity at the gates of rich men's houses?

A. It was.

Q. What was the rich man's crime?

A. "An unrelieved beggar at his gate."

Q. When this poor, diseased beggar died, what became of him?

A. (See verse 22.)

Q. What are we to understand when we read that Lazarus was "carried by the angels into Abraham's bosom"?

A. It is an expression that was used in those days by the Jews to describe "the rest of the faithful."

Q. Where do you find the history of Abraham, who was always so much reverenced by the Jewish people?

A. In Genesis, beginning at the twelfth chapter.

Q. The rich man is represented as dying, and being afterwards in hell; what is the word for "hell" in the original, and what is its signification?

A. The word is *Hades*, and it signifies *the place of the dead*, or the place where all the dead dwell together.

Q. Dives and Lazarus being thus represented in the

parable as being within sight of each other, and Dives being in torment, what does he ask?

A. (See verse 24.)

Q. Why should he say "*Father* Abraham"?

A. All the Jews recognized Abraham as the *father* of their nation.

Q. What reply is given to the rich man, and what reason is assigned for refusing his request?

A. (See verse 25.)

Q. However much some of us may suffer on earth more than others, and however unequal our lot may seem here, with regard to sickness, trouble, poverty, etc., what are we to believe respecting our future condition?

A. That we shall receive according to our faith.

Q. What other reason is assigned why Lazarus cannot comply with the request of the rich man?

A. (See verse 26.)

Q. Must not the good and the bad be forever really separated from each other, both in this world and the next?

A. They must be: their tastes are different; their affections are different; their enjoyments are different; their *hearts* are different; and however near their bodies may be to one another, *morally* and *spiritually* they can never be really united.

Q. What further request does Dives make?

A. (See verses 27 and 28.)

Q. What reply is made to it?

A. (See verses 29–31.)

Q. If we are not converted and sanctified with all the Christian opportunities and instructions that we are continually receiving, have we any right to ask for more?

A. We have not; for we have abundant means of

improving now, and we must be hard-hearted if we are not benefited by them.

Q. If all our religious advantages do not help us to be Christians, is it likely that we should be made so by seeing some of our friends who have died appear again among us?

A. We have no reason to believe that we should, and it would be vain and wicked in us to ask for it.

Q. Without dwelling on the reference Jesus may have had in this parable to the Jews and the Gentiles, and their comparative readiness to put faith in Him and His gospel, what is one great practical lesson that we may learn from it?

A. That under the Christian religion the rich and the poor are both judged according to their heart, and not according to their riches.

Q. If the poorest and the most afflicted here only have faith in God, what must be their condition?

A. They must have a peace of the soul, that on earth is worth far more than outward wealth; and in heaven, where no earthly riches can follow us, they will be blessed forever.

Q. If the rich are vicious, selfish, and worldly-minded, what must their condition be?

A. They must have an inward dissatisfaction and uneasiness which all their property cannot save them from, and hereafter they must suffer the fearful consequences of their sin.

Q. But may not the rich be pure, generous, and dear to Christ?

A. They may, if they will only make the effort, for God will help them. Abraham himself was rich. (Gen. xiii. 2.)

Q. What are the words of Scripture that best set forth the law respecting our future life?

A. "Whatsoever a man soweth, that shall he also reap." (Gal. vi. 7, 8.)

LESSON XXVI.

PARABLE OF THE MAN AND HIS SERVANT.

Q. WHAT are the Apostles said to have asked their Master to do for them, in St. Luke's Gospel, xvii. 5?

A. To increase their faith, so that they might be able to fulfill all the difficult duties which they would be called to perform as His followers.

Q. Who were the Apostles?

A. They were those whom Jesus chose and sent forth to plant His Church and proclaim His doctrines. (See St. Matt. x. 1–4, and Lesson II.)

Q. When they asked for more faith, what did they desire?

A. That they might have more trust in God, and a stronger attachment to Christ.

Q. What was the particular occasion of their making this petition?

A. They were probably afraid that the opposition and persecution of their enemies might tempt them to give up the preaching of Christ's doctrines, and forsake Him.

Q. What were some of the sufferings they actually endured afterwards, which put their faith to the trial?

A. They were driven from one place to another, shut up in prison, called by the most disgraceful names, accused of hating those whom they loved, and many of them were put to death in the most cruel and dreadful manner.

Q. Though our trials are different from theirs, is there not need for us also every day to lift a similar prayer?

A. There is; for every day we are tempted to sin in some way, and in every sin we forsake Christ.

Q. Why did the Apostles ask *Christ* to increase their faith?

A. Because they felt that whatever faith they had they received from Him.

Q. What reply did the Saviour make to their request?

A. (St. Luke xvii. 6.)

Q. This is evidently a figurative expression, not to be understood literally; what, then, is meant by it?

A. That if His followers have the right kind of faith, they shall be able to do things extremely difficult in resisting temptation and performing duty, — things as difficult otherwise, in a *moral* point of view, as pulling up a sycamine-tree is to the bodily strength, — and that the least real and vital faith has wonderful powers.

Q. In what other place does Jesus use a similar figure of speech, to show how strong a true Christian faith may become?

A. (St. Matthew xxi. 21.)

Q. Here (St. Luke xvii. 7) begins the parable of the man and his servant; what is the design of this parable?

A. To show that when we have done our utmost, and reached the strongest faith possible, we have done no more than we ought.

Q. When a man has a servant, does he expect to wait on the servant and to prepare his meals, or to have his servant wait on him?

A. Of course, to have the servant wait on him.

Q. Why?

A. Because he employs the servant, with a fair and honest understanding that this is to be his business.

Q. And if the servant does this, does he perform his duty to his employer?

A. He performs it exactly, and no more than his duty.

Q. What, then, is the reason that the employer does not think it necessary to thank the servant for such a service (verse 9)?

A. Because the terms of their agreement are only fulfilled, and the servant has not done a *favor*.

Q. What is the meaning of "I *trow* not"?

A. "I *think* not."

Q. What is the application Jesus makes of this parable to His followers?

A. (Verse 10.) He says, that so, when we have done our best, we have done no *favor* to the Almighty, over and above our duty, but just our duty, and no more.

Q. What is the meaning of the phrase, "unprofitable servants"?

A. Servants that have conferred no special obligations, though they may have been very useful in their work. (Job. xxxv. 7.)

Q. How does it appear that our obedience to God is no more than a servant's barely fulfilling his agreement with his master?

A. Because God has made us all that we are, and given us every thing we have, and, therefore, we owe to Him all that we can do.

Q. When we do right, do we not perform really as great a service to ourselves as to any one else?

A. We do; because we make ourselves happier and stronger.

Q. When we have accomplished our utmost at being good, is our goodness at all equal to God's kindness and love to us?

A. It never can be; for life, friends, health, joy, and faith are all His gifts.

Q. And yet, how can we best show our gratitude to God for the blessings we receive from Him?

A. By doing His will, and offering Him our prayers.

Q. But when we see that He is perfect, and infinitely greater and holier than we can be, how must we feel?

A. Very humble.

Q. If, then, our best actions, and the purest lives we can lead, are no more than what is due to our Maker, what should our continued effort be?

A. To render Him this our humble service, at least, cheerfully and constantly.

Q. How does this lesson make all wickedness appear?

A. As doubly disgraceful in us, and doubly ungrateful; for if goodness is no more than we owe to God, how much injustice and baseness are we guilty of when we do not render Him even that return!

Q. When our Father in heaven rewards us for doing well, is it because we earn that reward by any merit of our own?

A. Not at all; but because He loves us, and pours out blessings upon us, of His own free bounty, and for the sake of the righteousness of Christ, which we make ours by faith.

LESSON XXVII.

PARABLE OF THE UNJUST JUDGE.

Q. Where is the parable of the unjust judge recorded?

A. In the first eight verses of the eighteenth chapter of St. Luke's Gospel.

Q. In the first verse it is said Jesus spake this parable "unto *them*"; who were these persons?

A. His disciples. (St. Luke xvii. 22.)

Q. Is it probable this parable was a continuation of the discourse of Jesus recorded in the latter part of the preceding chapter?

A. It is; for we must remember that the division of the gospels into chapters was made for the convenience of the reader, and not to show that there was any interruption in what was said or done by Christ and His followers.

Q. What is the meaning of the phrase, "to this end"?

A. It means that Christ spoke the parable *for the purpose of teaching this particular lesson.*

Q. And what is this lesson?

A. He shows us that we ought to be in the habit of praying constantly; and that we should never be weary or discouraged in our prayers; that we should not, for any cause, omit to pray, because, if we persevere, our prayers will be answered.

Q. Does Jesus mean, in the second verse, to state it as a fact that there was really just such a judge as this?

A. He does not. He imagines such a person. It is

as if He should say, "Let us suppose there was in a city," &c.

Q. What was the office of such a "judge" as is here spoken of, in the time of our Saviour, and in His country?

A. There were actually three judges in every Jewish city;· and it was their business to decide questions about property, to settle difficulties and quarrels between the citizens, and to see that certain guilty persons were punished for their crimes.

Q. Had the judge, who is here imagined by Jesus, the character that such an important officer ought to have?

A. He had not; for while a judge ought by all means to fear and serve God, who is the Great Judge of all men, and ought to imitate His justice, and have a tender regard for the rights of his fellow-men, this one "feared not God, neither regarded man."

Q. What was the case presented to this wicked judge to decide?

A. A poor widow had been injured by an adversary, and she sought that what was her due might be restored to her.

Q. Was the judge willing to attend to her request, and grant her what justice required?

A. He was not at first; nor would he have been at all, for any regard to what was right and good, or any pity for her lonely condition.

Q. What finally induced him to give his attention to her case?

A. It was simply the fear that by her "continual coming" to seek his aid, she might occupy his time, or intrude upon his comfort, and so annoy him.

Q. What proof have we that she came to him more than once?

A. The word *came,* in the third verse, really signifies — in the Greek (the language in which this account was first written) — " she *kept coming.*"

Q. When the widow is represented as saying, "*Avenge* me," is it meant that she wished to have *revenge,* in a bad sense, and return evil for evil?

A. Not at all. With that meaning the parable would be very hard to understand. If that had been her request, she *ought* to have been denied.

Q. What, then, did she ask for?

A. She asked — as we find by ascertaining the signification of the word that is translated *avenge* — only that she might have justice done her by a person who had wronged her.

Q. Did the judge do any thing that was honorable or kind, or any thing that could be acceptable in the sight of God, when he granted her request?

A. He did not; for although he did what was right in itself, yet, as he did it for the sake of his own ease, he acted from a selfish motive.

Q. What would have been a noble and pure motive?

A. The religious love of doing right, or a regard to the poor widow.

Q. What is the meaning of the Saviour's explanation of this parable in verses 7 and 8?

A. That if even this unjust judge was persuaded to listen to the widow, against his inclinations, merely on account of her importuning him, how much more reason have we to believe that God, who is perfectly just and perfectly kind, will hear and answer the prayers of the children whom He loves!

Q. Who are intended by the "elect," in the 7th verse?

A. Those early Christians who, because they believed on Christ and followed Him, were called God's "elect," — that is, His "chosen ones." (St. Matt. xxiv. 31, and St. Mark xiii. 20, 22, 27.)

Q. How do you understand the latter part of the 8th verse?

A. Jesus there mentions the danger lest, when a fair opportunity shall be given for the preaching of His gospel, few will be found on earth ready to receive it, and to have faith in Him and in His words.

Q. But has not the parable a more general application?

A. It contains important truth that is applicable to every Christian, — to each one of us.

Q. Will you name one inference we are to draw from it?

A. That we should all be as anxious for spiritual blessings from God, and as constant and urgent in our prayers for His help in renewing our hearts and improving our characters, as we are to have justice done us in business transactions.

Q. Will you mention another great truth that we are taught by this parable?

A. We are taught that God will surely hear those who earnestly call upon Him, — who are willing to "cry day and night unto Him."

Q. Will you repeat the first part of what was said to be the chief lesson Jesus teaches here?

A. He encourages us to be in the habit of praying constantly; "that we ought always to pray and not to faint."

Q. Can you name and repeat some other passages in

the New Testament, where this duty of "praying always" is enjoined?

A. St. Luke xxi. 36; Romans xii. 12; Colossians iv. 2; and 1 Thessalonians v. 17.

Q. What do you understand, in these texts, by "praying always," and "praying without ceasing?"

A. That we ought all to pray to God very frequently, every day we live, and thus maintain that devout disposition, that trustful state of the mind, which *never ceases,* and which nothing but prayer can produce in us.

Q. Will you mention some reasons why you should so pray?

A. Because we depend on God for *every thing* we have, — for all our possessions, our friends, our pleasures, our knowledge, our virtues, and our hopes of heaven; because we thus please God, and keep His commandments; because we thus prove to Him that we are sincere in loving Him and trusting Him; because our communion with Him must purify our souls, cleanse our hearts from bad passions and evil desires, enable us to keep all our best resolutions; to be useful to our fellow-men, and give us inward strength and peace.

Q. What is the other part of the chief lesson of this parable?

A. That we need never be weary or discouraged in our prayers.

Q. In what other texts of the New Testament are we shown that we should *wait patiently* for our Heavenly Father to hear us and bless us?

A. St. James v. 7, 8; Hebrews x. 36; 2 Thessalonians iii. 5; St. Luke xxi. 19.

Q. How does it happen that we often become discouraged in our prayers?

A. We are impatient, and in haste for some visible answer, instead of submitting entirely to the loving will of God.

Q. Can we expect to know the best *method* in which our petitions shall be fulfilled?

A. We cannot. We ought to believe that God will answer us *in some way*, though the answer may be invisible, spiritual, in the secret benefits of the soul.

Q. What should be our feeling when we supplicate earthly blessings?

A. We should feel, that to receive precisely what we ask for *might* be the most serious evil, and therefore we should be willing to leave all results with Him who careth for us as a parent, adding to our other requests, "Father, Thy will, not mine, be done!"

Q. What is a great encouragement to us to continue our endeavors to pray, in a reverential and humble spirit, even when we begin to be disheartened?

A. The cheering fact that the more we engage in devotion, the more delightful does it become, while our compassionate Father never fails to listen to the sincere cry of His children.

Q. What is the true way for a Christian to regard prayer?

A. As his dearest privilege, since it brings him to his Lord and his Lord to him.

LESSON XXVIII.

PARABLE OF THE PUBLICAN AND THE PHARISEE.

Q. WHERE do you find the parable of the publican and the Pharisee?

A. In St. Luke xviii. 9–14.

Q. For whose benefit and instruction was it especially designed?

A. (See verse 9.)

Q. What was the object of the Pharisees in their prayers?

A. To make themselves *appear* pious to other men, but not to commune with God, or be made holier.

Q. What did they think the excellence of a prayer consisted in?

A. In its length, and in the sanctimonious air with which it is offered.

Q. What were they soon guilty of, accordingly?

A. Insincerity, and often the basest hypocrisy.

Q. What does the excellence of prayer *really* consist in?

A. In the feeling of humility, penitence, and simple faith which is in the heart when the prayer is made.

Q. How does Jesus illustrate this contrast between a true prayer and a false one?

A. By giving an example of both, in this parable.

Q. What was the office of a "publican," or tax-gatherer?

A. (See Lesson XXII.)

Q. What was the Pharisee's prayer in fact, as it is given in verse 11?

A. It was a vain boast of his own goodness.

Q. Are we to understand, of course, that this person was as good as he represented himself to be?

A. Not by any means; in those points in which men think themselves to be strong, they are very apt to be weak.

Q. Suppose that he had been as good as he thought himself, would his goodness, even according to his own account, have been of the highest kind?

A. It would not; for, on the one hand, he would only be free from certain flagrant vices, and, on the other, he would be scrupulous about certain outward ceremonies. He might be all this, and yet be quite empty of benevolence and kindness, or an earnest love for God.

Q. Is it sufficient for us, in the sight of God, that we can say we are no worse than others?

A. It is not; we should have a higher standard.

Q. Is it enough that we are able to say we do no *harm* to others?

A. It is not; for we ought to do a great deal of good to others.

Q. Did the Pharisees think it a great merit to fast twice in the week?

A. They did, — on Mondays and Thursdays.

Q. What was it to give " tithes of all that he possessed "?

A. To pay a certain proportion (a tenth) of his property, as a sort of tax, for religious purposes. (See Lesson XVII., and Deut. xiv. 22.)

Q. When do we make a right use of church-ceremonies and particular days like a fast?

A. When we employ them heartily.

Q. When do we make a wrong and false use of them.

A. When we make them stand *instead* of a holy heart, and employ them to excuse ourselves from other duties.

Q. Can such things as these ever be *substitutes* for faith, or release us, in the sight of God, from performing all our daily duties?

A. Never. (St. Matt. xxiii. 23.)

Q. As the Pharisee gives us an example of pride and disgusting self-admiration, what does the publican give us an example of in his prayer?

A. Of humility and beautiful penitence and devotion.

Q. What is implied (verse 13) by his "standing afar off"?

A. That he did not wish to thrust himself into notice, as the Pharisees did (St. Matt. vi. 5), but to retire out of sight.

Q. How does the same humility appear in the next clause?

A. He "would not lift up so much as his eyes unto heaven," but fixed them on the ground — a token of his lowliness before God.

Q. How does the same humble sense of unworthiness appear yet farther?

A. In the next expression, — he "smote upon his breast," — a movement indicating self-reproach and sorrow.

Q. But how is this humility manifested yet more clearly?

A. In the prayer he breathes to God, where he confesses that he is a sinner, and entreats forgiveness: — "God be merciful to me a sinner." "*Me;*" 1 Tim. i. 15.

Q. What may we learn from this?

A. That our prayers should be offered in lowliness of spirit.

Q. What reason do we find for this in the next verse?

A. Jesus assures us, on His own authority, that whoever prays thus will be justified in the sight of God, rather than the one who *pretends* to pray, with pharisaic pride in his heart.

Q. What is the meaning of the word "justified" here?

A. "Looked upon as having a right heart, and, therefore, forgiven."

Q. In the brief *moral* that is appended to this parable in verse 14, what is said of every person who "exalteth himself," that is, praises himself, and thinks too highly of himself?

A. That he "shall be abased," that is, a low place will be given him in the esteem of mankind, who will soon find out his real worth, and in the unerring judgment of God.

Q. On the other hand, how will it be with those who *humble themselves*, or feel their deficiencies, and cherish a lowly temper?

A. They "shall be exalted," in the high regard of good men, and in the favor of God. (See verse 17.)

Q. When we pray, what should we remember?

A. That He sees the secrets of our hearts, and that we cannot possibly deceive Him.

Q. What, then, may we always do without fear?

A. Confess all our faults, and beseech Him to pardon them.

LESSON XXIX.

PARABLE OF THE TEN POUNDS.

Q. WHERE and when did our Lord deliver the parable of the ten pounds?

A. On His last journey to Jerusalem. (See St. Luke xix. 1.)

Q. Where do you find the occasion and object of this parable stated?

A. In verse 11th.

Q. What was the occasion of it?

A. Jesus saw that His disciples expected Him to make Himself a king, according to the old notion of the Jewish people, and establish an earthly empire, with power and splendor.

Q. What did He teach them respecting this expectation?

A. That it was false, and that He had no such intention at His first coming.

Q. What did He always tell them was His great purpose?

A. To redeem them from sin, and make them *better* in heart and life, — not richer, or more favored in political privileges, or any outward condition.

Q. What kind of a "kingdom," then, did He wish to establish?

A. A spiritual kingdom, coming with power, built and felt in the soul, and embodied in the Church of the Living God.

Q. What does Jesus show respecting this *kingdom*, in the parable before us?

A. That it is offered to all alike; and that just according as men use or neglect the light and truth given them in Him shall they be blessed or be miserable.

Q. What is the story of the parable?

A. A certain nobleman, expecting to be made the prince or king of the country where he lives, goes to a distant place to receive the office from a higher government.

Q. Was this actually done in Judea?

A. It was; the ruler of that country went to Rome to secure his office, for Judea was under the control of the Roman emperor.

Q. What is the nobleman said to do before he starts on this journey?

A. (Verse 13.)

Q. What was the value of one of these pounds, or *minas*?

A. Probably about twenty dollars.

Q. What is the meaning of " *Occupy* till I come "?

A. "*Use* this money,— invest it in trade to increase its amount."

Q. What took place after this nobleman departed?

A. (Verse 14.) A remonstrance was sent to the emperor by the people, urging him not to appoint this nobleman as the prince.

Q. Was the remonstrance successful?

A. It appears not, from verse 15.

Q. On the nobleman's return to his country, as a prince, what did he do?

A. (Verse 15.)

Q. The ten servants having received at the beginning a pound, or *mina*, each, to trade with, what does the first of them say he has gained by trading with his?

A. (Verse 16.)

Q. How does the newly-appointed prince reward him, in distributing the offices of his government?

A. (Verse 17.) He gives him the place of a subordinate governor over ten cities.

Q. What happened in relation to the second servant?

A. (Verses 18, 19.)

Q. What appears respecting the third servant in verses 20 and 21?

A. That he had been idle, and thought ill of his master.

Q. How did the prince treat him for his indolence and unfaithfulness?

A. (Verses 22–24.)

Q. Does the prince admit that he was really an austere, or hard and exacting man, in verse 22?

A. He does not; he only says to the servant, If you thought me so, your duty was, for that very reason, to be industrious, and prepare for a reckoning with me.

Q. What is verse 25?

A. It is a remark thrown in by some person standing by,—surprised that the one talent this servant had should be taken from him and given to the one who had ten talents already.

Q. How does Jesus reply to this remark, and defend the conduct of the prince in this particular?

A. He says (verse 26), that those who apply themselves earnestly to their duty shall not only retain what they have, but gain more; while those who are careless will lose what little they may have. (See also St. Luke viii. 18.)

Q. Who are the persons alluded to in verse 27 who are so awfully punished?

A. They are "enemies" mentioned in verse 14.

Q. Whom, now, does Jesus represent by the "nobleman," or prince, in this parable?

A. Himself, as the author of the gospel, that is, as the head, or prince, of the spiritual kingdom of righteousness and truth.

Q. Who are the "servants"?

A. All who are acquainted with the gospel of Christ.

Q. What is the pound committed to every one of these servants?

A. This gospel of Christ and His salvation.

Q. When was Christ disowned in the terms of the parable?

A. At the crucifixion. (St. John xix. 15.)

Q. What, then, are you to learn from this parable?

A. That in proportion as I improve my religious advantages, with faith in the Saviour, I shall be blessed.

Q. Suppose you do not improve your opportunities, but are careless, selfish, and disobedient?

A. Then I am taught here that what little peace and comfort I have in my soul must grow less and less, till nothing is left me but remorse, anguish, and sorrow of heart.

Q. Who are those that must expect the awful fate pointed out in verse 27?

A. Those who will not try to lead Christian lives, believing and following Christ.

Q. What fearful event did Jesus probably allude to, which happened soon after that time?

A. The destruction of Jerusalem, when multitudes of those who would not believe on Him, and be His disciples, were killed and burnt by the Roman armies.

Q. How is the lesson of this parable encouraging?

A. It shows us that no faith we can gain will be lost, or fail of being a source of good to us.

Q. How is it solemn?

A. It shows us that our condition here and hereafter depends on our characters.

LESSON XXX.

THE PARABLE OF THE TWO SONS.

Q. What course did Jesus take after He delivered the parable of the last lesson?

A. (St. Luke xix. 28; St. John xii. 1–14.)

Q. What great feast were many Jews going up to Jerusalem at this time to attend?

A. The Feast of the Passover. (St. John xi. 55.)

Q. What was the Passover among the Jews?

A. It was a feast kept by that nation at the time of the year which with us is the Spring; the same that the Church keeps at Easter, to celebrate the death and resurrection of Christ. (See 1 Cor. v. 7, 8.)

Q. What was the object of it?

A. To commemorate the night when their ancestors escaped from their bondage under Pharaoh, in Egypt, and commenced their journey towards Palestine, which was afterwards their home. (Exod. xii.)

Q. What especial mercy did God show that night to the Jews, or Israelites, which gave its name to this feast?

A. While God destroyed the eldest child in every family of the Egyptians, for their wickedness, he *passed over*, or spared, the families of the Israelites, whom He did not wish to punish.

Q. After the arrival of Jesus at Jerusalem, how does it appear that He spent the days?

A. Teaching in the Temple. (See St. Matt. xxi. 1-9, and St. Mark xi. 11; also on the next day, St. Matt. xxi. 10-17; also on the day after, St. Matt. xxi. 23.)

Q. When was this parable of the two sons delivered?

A. On the last of the days just mentioned (see St. Matt. xxi. 23-32), as He was teaching in the great Temple.

Q. With whom does it appear that Jesus passed the nights at this time?

A. With His friends, Lazarus, Mary, and Martha, at Bethany. (See St. Matt. xxi. 17, and St. Mark xi. 11.)

Q. What led to this parable of the two sons?

A. A conversation of Jesus with the chief priests and elders, related in verse 23, &c., of St. Matt. xxi.

Q. What was the character of these "chief priests and elders"?

A. The same with that described as belonging to the "scribes and Pharisees," in Lesson XXII.

Q. What was their error?

A. Supposing that fasting, and paying tithes, and disputing with each other about questions that had no connection with character, were things of more consequence than benevolence, justice, and piety.

Q. In the parable (verse 28), a man is supposed to have two sons of different characters; what does he request one of them to do?

A. To go and labor in his vineyard, or garden of grapes.

Q. What reply did this son make?

A. (Verse 29.)

Q. What, may we suppose, had been the character of this son?

A. Up to this time he had been disobedient and self-willed, as appears from his rude answer to his father.

Q. What probably induced him afterwards to repent of that answer, and go to the work?

A. He reflected on his duties to his father, and was ashamed to disobey him, or refuse his request.

Q. What is the father represented as saying to the other son?

A. (Verse 30.)

Q. What was the character of this son?

A. He did not keep his promise; he *pretended* to be obedient, but ran away from his duty.

Q. Whom did Jesus intend to describe under the character of this second son?

A. The scribes and Pharisees, the chief priests and elders.

Q. Why?

A. Because they *professed* to be righteous, but were not. (Verses 31, 32.)

Q. How are we in danger of being like them?

A. If we are good only in our own estimation, but do not strive constantly to live for Christ.

Q. When we form a good resolution only to break it soon, how is our character apt to be affected?

A. To be hardened in sin, and led farther astray from duty.

Q. Having committed ourselves to a right course, either openly or in our own minds, what should we apply all our energies to do?

A. To persevere in it, resolutely and nobly.

Q. Wherein are you to imitate the *first-mentioned* son?

A. Not in refusing to do my duty at first, but in really performing it, both towards my earthly parents and towards my Father in heaven.

Q. If you have foolishly refused to do right, what is the first thing to be done?

A. To repent, to feel humble sorrow, and to go straight to perform that which I have hitherto neglected.

Q. Who, then, are described by Jesus under the character of the first-mentioned son?

A. Those who are sinful and thoughtless for a time, but who afterwards sincerely turn to a Christian course of life.

Q. What does Jesus uniformly teach shall become of such persons?

A. They shall be forgiven, accepted, and blessed by our Heavenly Father.

Q. What course can you point out that would have been far better than that pursued by either of these two sons?

A. To have said, "I will go, sir," and then to have gone to the Christian labor cheerfully, and industriously performing it, would have been the beautiful and worthy conduct of a truly filial and dutiful child.

Q. How, then, would you draw from that example your right conduct towards God?

A. I should never hesitate to follow His commandments, but always find satisfaction in doing His will.

LESSON XXXI.

PARABLE OF THE VINEYARD LET OUT TO HUSBANDMEN.

Q. When was this parable spoken?
A. Immediately after that contained in the last lesson, and while Jesus was teaching in the temple, the Tuesday before His crucifixion.

Q. Where do you find it?
A. In St. Matt. xxi. 33, &c., and also in St. Mark xii. 1–9, and St. Luke xx. 9–16.

Q. What is the householder represented by Jesus as doing?
A. (Verse 33.)

Q. What part of the "wine-press" was the "vat"?
A. It was a tub, in which the wine was received after it was trodden out of the grapes that grew in the vineyard.

Q. What was the "tower" built for?
A. As a post of observation, to guard the vineyard from all kinds of depredation.

Q. The householder, being still absent when the fruit became ripe, does what?
A. (Verse 34.)

Q. How do the husbandmen, to whom he intrusted the care of the vineyard, treat the servants whom he now sends for the fruit?
A. (Verses 35, 36.)

Q. But what right had the householder to these fruits?
A. He had "let out" the vineyard to these husband-

men, and according to customs then prevailing he was to receive a certain portion of the fruits as the *rent*.

Q. What was the object of these wicked and cruel husbandmen, in so treating these servants?

A. To avoid giving up what they owed to the householder, and keep all to themselves.

Q. How did the owner suppose they would regard his own son?

A. (Verse 37.)

Q. What object had the husbandmen in putting him to death?

A. To secure not only the fruits of the season, but the vineyard itself, by destroying him who was to inherit it. (Verses 38, 39.)

Q. Jesus, after relating the parable thus far, asks those who hear Him what must be expected to be done to those wicked husbandmen, by the owner, or "lord," of the vineyard, — and what is their reply?

A. (Verse 41.)

Q. How did they commit themselves, unknowingly, by this answer?

A. They might not have perceived that the very meaning of the parable was a bitter reproof of themselves.

Q. How was it so?

A. Jesus meant these rulers of the Jews, by the "husbandmen" whom He described.

Q. Who, then, was the "householder," or "lord of the vineyard"?

A. The Creator. (Is. v. 1.)

Q. What were the "fruits" due to Him from His people, the Jews?

A. Fruitful and holy lives.

Q. Did they yield Him those fruits?

A. They did not; but when messengers came to teach them faithfulness and holiness, they persecuted or slew them.

Q. Who were these messengers, or teachers, or "servants," that God sent, from time to time, to recall the Jews to their duty?

A. Prophets and wise men, such as Elijah, Samuel, Isaiah, &c. (2 Chron. xxxvi. 15.)

Q. Were such persons actually put to death by the Jews?

A. They were. (See 1 Kings xviii. 13; Jer. xxxviii. 6; Heb. xi. 32, 37; and St. Luke xi. 50–51.)

Q. Who was "the son," that was at last sent?

A. Jesus Christ, the dearly beloved Son of God.

Q. What, then, was the blindest sin of all in the Jews?

A. That they put to death that Son of God; that they crucified the Saviour of the world.

Q. What passage does Jesus apply to Himself from the Psalms?

A. (Ps. cxviii. 22, 23.)

Q. Why does Jesus compare Himself to a stone rejected by the masons as unfit for use, yet afterwards found worthy to be the head-stone at the corner of the building?

A. Because He was at first to be rejected and slain by the Jews, but afterwards to be the Head of the whole Christian Church, honored and reverenced as the Saviour of men.

Q. How was the warning of verse 43 fulfilled on the Jews?

A. A few years after, their nation was destroyed, their

chief city was leveled to the ground, and the "kingdom" was "taken from" them.

Q. What is the meaning of Christ's language in verse 44?

A. Whoever shall resist Christ and His truth shall come to nothing; and whoever, by willful sin, shall expose himself to the judgments of Christ's religion, shall be terribly destroyed by them. (Heb. x. 25-31.)

Q. How did the Pharisees feel (verses 45, 46), when they saw that Jesus was rebuking them by His parables?

A. They wished to take vengeance on Him, but dared not, because a multitude believed and followed Him.

Q. How should we all feel respecting our lives in this world?

A. That we owe the "fruits" of them to our Heavenly Father, and that He has a right to our service.

Q. When we see that He is sending us messengers and teachers of so many kinds, what should our disposition be?

A. To be persuaded by all that we feel, and hear, and see, and suffer, to put our whole faith in God, and do His will faithfully.

Q. What should we feel to be the one thing that should draw our gratitude most perfectly to God?

A. The gift of His Son, Jesus Christ, who came to live and suffer, and be reproached, and put to death on earth, that He might bring us to Eternal Life.

Q. What is the least service we can render to show our gratitude for such mercy?

A. (Rom. xii. 1.)

LESSON XXXII.

PARABLE OF THE MARRIAGE-FEAST.

Q. WHERE was Jesus when He uttered the parable of the marriage-feast?

A. He was in Jerusalem, at the great Temple, on Tuesday of Holy Week.

Q. Where do you find this parable?

A. In the first fourteen verses of the 22d chapter of St. Matthew.

Q. What other parable of our Lord that you have studied closely resembles this?

A. The parable of the Great Supper, in St. Luke xiv. 10–24, spoken on a different occasion.

Q. It appears from verses 2 and 3 that a king is spoken of here as having made a marriage, or marriage-feast, for his son; what can you say of such feasts in the time of the Saviour?

A. Marriage-feasts, among the Jews, and in the time of Christ, were very splendid. Whenever a rich person was married, great preparations were made; costly dishes were provided, and a large number of guests were invited.

Q. How long did these wedding festivals sometimes continue?

A. Seven days.

Q. It seems, from verse 3, that this king sent *two* invitations to the guests; was this customary?

A. It was; one was sent a considerable time beforehand; and then, just before the wedding, servants were sent out to call the guests in. (Esther vi. 14.)

Q. What do you say of the kindness of this king in sending out a third time, when his previous invitations had been scorned?

A. It left them no excuse for not coming.

Q. Read verse 4, to see what his message was this time; what were "fatlings"?

A. Fatted beasts, killed for the dinner.

Q. Did the persons who were invited pay any attention to this last message?

A. They did not (see verse 5); and some of them were so ungrateful and cruel as to abuse and destroy the servants that brought it.

Q. What is the meaning of "*entreated* them spitefully"?

A. "*Treated* them spitefully, or maliciously"; *entreat* does not mean here *beseech*, as with us.

Q. Was it considered as peculiarly insulting, among the Jews, to whom Christ was now speaking, to neglect or refuse to attend a wedding?

A. It was; more so than among us.

Q. What did the king do to punish this wickedness?

A. (See verse 7.)

Q. What did he do next?

A. (See verses 8 and 9.)

Q. As the invited guests had refused to come, who now had the privilege of attending the feast?

A. The poor, strangers, and beggars from the highways. (See verse 10.)

Q. What was the "wedding-garment," which the man mentioned in verse 11 had not on?

A. It was a robe, which every guest was required to put on before he went in to the feast.

Q. When this man was called to account for having

come in his common clothes, without this robe, why was he "speechless"?

A. Because he had no good excuse to offer for doing so.

Q. But if these guests were poor people, brought in from the streets, was it not unreasonable to suppose that they had the means of furnishing themselves with such a garment?

A. Not at all; for it was the custom of persons who gave such entertainments to provide gifts for the guests, and to furnish garments without expense. (2 Kings v. 5.)

Q. How do we learn this?

A. Travellers and historians, well acquainted with the habits of the Jews, have told us so. Some rich men had hundreds, or even thousands, of these garments, ready for use in their houses. (Esther ii. 18.)

Q. What reason, then, could this man have had for not putting on such a robe?

A. He was either shamefully careless, or else he was willing to disoblige and insult the king, and offend the rest of the company, by appearing in a singular and mean dress, and refusing the gift.

Q. What method did the king take to reprove this man's impudence?

A. He ordered him to be "bound," so that he could not resist, and then to be taken away from the feast.

Q. What is meant when it is said he was to be cast into "outer darkness"?

A. These feasts were held in the evening, and the man was taken from the bright light of the illuminated apartments into the darkness out of doors.

Q. Why is it said "there shall be weeping and gnashing of teeth"?

A. The man would be so disappointed and mortified at being punished and turned out of the feast, that he would weep with rage, and gnash his teeth in anger.

Q. Will you state now the Saviour's object in relating this story?

A. To show that many who have had a free opportunity have yet willfully and wickedly refused to enter into the "kingdom of heaven." (See verse 2.)

Q. When He compares this feast to the "kingdom of heaven," what does He signify?

A. To understand and believe His teachings, and to live as they direct us to live, is to belong to His "kingdom," or His "Church," and this is a feast

Q. Is not this a feast much more precious than any other?

A. It ought to be regarded so, for it is a spiritual feast, and it lasts forever.

Q. Who is the "king" that spreads before us every day this feast?

A. God, our Father.

Q. Who are the "servants" that God sends to invite us to this feast?

A. The holy Apostles, and all ministers of the gospel.

Q. To whom did the Apostles offer to teach that truth first?

A. To the Jewish nation, to which they themselves belonged.

Q. How did these Jews receive the offer?

A. They would not believe, but they persecuted and put to death those who attempted to teach them, like the bad men in the parable.

Q. How was verse 7 fulfilled in the case of these Jews?

A. The "armies" of the Romans came, a few years after, and "destroyed" as many as *eleven hundred thousand Jews,* and "burned up their city," Jerusalem.

Q. Whom are we to understand by those in the "highways," that were afterwards invited to the privileges of the Church?

A. The men of all other nations, "bad and good," not Jews. (See Acts xiii. 46, 47, and St. Matt. viii. 11.)

Q. What excuses are we apt to make for not regarding Christ's invitation?

A. We foolishly pretend that we have not time, when we have time; or, more often, we neglect Him, because we are too much taken up with worldly thoughts and amusements, as the men in the parable were with their "farms" and their "merchandise."

Q. What is the Bride of Christ?

A. The Bride is the Church. (Eph. v. 25–27; Rev. xxii. 17, and xix. 9.)

Q. How can you apply to yourself what is said of the man that had not on "a wedding-garment"?

A. We can only "come holy and clean to the heavenly feast" of the Lord's Supper below, or of the Marriage Supper in heaven, by having our Saviour's righteousness, put on by faith and love. (Isaiah lxiv. 5, and lxi. 10; Rev. xix. 8.)

LESSON XXXIII.

PARABLE OF THE TEN VIRGINS.

Q. Where does it appear that the parable of the virgins must have been spoken by Jesus?

A. On the Mount of Olives, a height of ground near Jerusalem, whither he retired after delivering the preceding parables in the Temple. (See St. Matt. xxiv. 3.)

Q. Where is it written?

A. In St. Matt. xxv. 1–12.

Q. What reason have you to suppose that it was a part of the discourse of the Saviour recorded in the previous chapter?

A. It begins with the word "*Then,*" as if it were a continuation of what goes before; and, besides, the *subject* is the same.

Q. What is that subject?

A. Jesus is urging on His followers the duty of *watchfulness*, the duty of being *prepared* for a great change (xxiv. 42).

Q. What does He call the whole of His followers in verse 1?

A. The "kingdom of heaven."

Q. What does He compare them to?

A. To a band of maidens going out to join the bridegroom at a wedding. (Ps. xlv. 15.)

Q. What custom is alluded to here, which prevailed among the Jews?

A. Their weddings were observed with much parade; the bridegroom marched to the house of the bride's father, and having received the bride at her home, this procession again marched to the bridegroom's house, with music, torches, and great gayety.

Q. Is this custom still kept up in Eastern countries?

A. It is.

Q. What were the "lamps"?

A. They resembled torches, and were used to make a brilliant display, — these weddings being held in the night.

Q. Why are a part of these young women who went out to meet the bridegroom said to have been "wise"?

A. Because, as they did not know the time when the bridegroom would arrive, they had the prudence and forethought to take oil enough to keep their lamps burning (verse 4).

Q. Why were the others "foolish"?

A. Because they took so little oil that it was burnt out while they were waiting for the bridegroom (verse 3).

Q. As they all waited at a certain point, what happened in consequence of the bridegroom's delay?

A. They all fell asleep (verse 5).

Q. When at last, at midnight, the bridegroom approached, what took place?

A. They awaked, and made ready to receive him (verses 6 and 7).

Q. What did the foolish virgins say to the wise?

A. (Verse 8.)

Q. What reply was made to them?

A. (Verse 9.)

Q. How did these careless and foolish virgins learn the folly of not being prepared beforehand?

A. They returned too late with their oil, and were shut out from the wedding-feast, because they were not in the procession (verse 10).

Q. What did they cry out, in their disappointment?

A. "Open to us," and allow us to come in.

Q. What reply did the bridegroom make to them?

A. "I know you not"; that is, "I have not seen you in the procession of my friends, and, therefore, I cannot admit you to the supper."

Q. How does Jesus apply the lesson of this parable to His disciples?

LESSONS ON THE PARABLES. 151

A. He says, "Watch, therefore, for ye know neither the day nor the hour wherein the Son of Man cometh" (verse 13).

Q. Whom does the Saviour mean by the "Son of Man"?

A. Himself.

Q. What time does He refer to here, as the "coming of the Son of Man"?

A. His reappearance, in power and great glory, to take the Kingdom and reign visibly and personally on the earth. (Zech. xiv. 4–9; 1 Thess. iv. 16; Rev. xix. 7.)

Q. Does the gospel tell us when the time of this "coming again in His glorious majesty" shall be?

A. It fixes no time; but the Saviour says it shall be before "this generation shall pass away."

Q. What, then, is meant by "this generation?"

A. The Jewish people.

Q. At what season of the Church-year is the doctrine of Christ's second coming or advent, brought specially to mind?

A. At the Advent season; because the first and second comings are naturally associated together, — the second being the fulfillment of the first. (See Collect for First Sunday in Advent.)

Q. To those of us that are to die before the time of that future coming, where will be the Christian's vision of Christ?

A. In the other world, after death.

Q. How is that meeting regarded by the Apostles, in their great love for their Redeemer?

A. As the most inspiring and joyful of all the expected events of their life. (Phil. i. 23.)

Q. Practically, how ought the time of Christ's appearing always to be regarded?

A. As near at hand. (Phil. iv. 5; 1 Thess. v. 1, 2, 23; 1 Pet. iv. 7; Rev. xxii. 20.)

Q. What is the right preparation for it?

A. Faithful love and service *here* to our Lord, who is to appear to gather His own to Himself. (2 Pet. i. 10.)

Q. What will make you like the foolish virgins?

A. To be unprepared, "asleep," thinking only of other things, or caring nothing for our Lord and His spiritual kingdom. (St. Matt. xiii. 5.)

Q. What door will be shut against you then?

A. The door of repentance and faith, which is the door of heaven.

Q. And since you do not know what may happen the next hour or moment, what is your first duty?

A. To "watch" always; to be ready *now*. (See 1 Thess. v. 6.) Serving Christ is going out to meet the Bridegroom.

———◆———

LESSON XXXIV.

PARABLE OF THE TALENTS.

Q. What words, in the opinion of learned students of the Scriptures, may be put in the place of the expression "the kingdom of heaven," in St. Matt. xxv. 14?

A. *The Son of Man*, that is, the Saviour, in whom the whole "kingdom of heaven" is included and embodied.

Q. What does Jesus then go on to compare Himself to, in the parable of the talents?

A. (Verse 14.)

Q. What is this man represented as doing, when he leaves home?

A. (Verses 14 and 15.)

Q. What was his object in this?

A. He wished his property to be put to a good use and increased during his absence.

Q. How much was a "talent"?

A. Its exact value in our money is not determined, but it amounted to more than a thousand dollars.

Q. How did he who received the largest sum in trust deal with it?

A. (Verse 16.)

Q. And how did he who received the next smaller sum, or two talents, deal with his trust?

A. (Verse 17.)

Q. What did he who received the smallest sum do?

A. (Verse 18.)

Q. Will you describe what took place when the master or "lord" came and reckoned with the *first* of these servants?

A. (Verses 20 and 21.)

Q. What is meant by the expression "Enter thou into the joy of thy lord"?

A. "Enter into the enjoyment of the blessings which your master will give you for your faithfulness."

Q. What took place when the *second* servant was reckoned with?

A. (Verses 22 and 23.)

Q. What account did the *third* servant have to give?

A. (Verse 24.)

Q. What severe sentence does the master pronounce on this idle and unprofitable servant?

A. (Verses 26–30.)

Q. Does the master mean to admit (verse 26) that he was a hard, unfeeling, and unreasonable person, as the servant had accused him of being?

A. He does not; but only to say that, if this was the servant's opinion, he ought certainly to have been more faithful, and more ready to give account.

Q. What is the meaning of "usury," in verse 27?

A. "Interest" on the money; or, rather, the *proceeds* which the money would have brought, if it had been properly invested and employed.

Q. Why was it just that the talent should be taken from this servant, and given to the faithful one?

A. Because the faithful one had shown that he could turn it to a good use.

Q. What feeling do the terms "weeping and gnashing of teeth" indicate?

A. Shame, disappointment, and intense anguish.

Q. How is this parable related to that of the ten virgins?

A. This teaches us active Christian duties; that one contemplative: this working for Christ; that watching and waiting for Him. (St. Mark xiii. 34.)

Q. What other parable does this one very much resemble?

A. That of the ten pounds.

Q. In what does this differ from that?

A. In that, the same sum was given to each of the servants; while in this, the sum in every case is different.

Q. What are we reminded of by this circumstance in this parable of the talents?

A. That every human being has his own peculiar gifts or talents. (Eph. iv. 8–12.)

Q. What was doubtless the design of the Creator in producing this variety among His children?

A. To render mankind useful in different ways, so that all important works might be done.

Q. Looking at your companions, what are some of the "talents" that different individuals among them are intrusted with?

A. One has an excellent memory; another, ingenuity; another, a strong and healthy body; another, riches.

Q. What has every one?

A. Something by which he can do good and please God.

Q. By whom are *all* these gifts bestowed upon us?

A. By our Heavenly Father. (1 Cor. xii. 4.)

Q. What is further taught us in the parable?

A. That for every power or faculty we have, of body or mind, and for every opportunity, we shall be called to account by the great Giver, just as the servants were called to reckon with their master. (Eccl. xi. 9.)

Q. What is further taught here?

A. That those who have little property, or leisure, or intellect, are just as really accountable for *what they have*, as those that possess more of these things.

Q. Shall we be held accountable at last for the amount of what was given us at our birth, or only for the use we shall have made of it?

A. Only for the use we shall have made of it.

Q. What appears from verse 29?

A. The more good we do, the more shall we be able to do, and the more shall we love to do it.

Q. What is equally true on the other hand?

A. The more we indulge ourselves in any kind of sin, the harder will it be to resist temptation.

Q. If this is the case, what ought you to resolve and strive to do?

A. To resist the beginnings of evil in my mind.

Q. What glorious and animating promise is held out to you in verses 21 and 23?

A. I am told that for every little thing in which I am conscientious and dutiful, I shall receive a great blessing from my Father in heaven.

Q. But if you are idle and complaining, and do not *use* every power of doing good, what have you to fear?

A. The dreadful punishment of the "unprofitable servant."

LESSON XXXV.

PARABLE OF THE SHEEP AND THE GOATS.

Q. WHAT gives a peculiar interest and solemnity to this parable of the sheep and the goats?

A. It was the last parable uttered by the Saviour, being delivered by Him just before His trial and crucifixion. (St. Matt. xxvi. 1–2.)

Q. How is it connected with the passages and parables preceding it?

A. From the verse that introduces it (St. Matt. xxv. 31) we learn that the subject is the same that was begun in chapter xxiv., the "coming of the Son of Man."

Q. What have we seen that "coming" to be?

A. His actual descent from heaven to reign on earth.

Q. Is there not great appropriateness in His speaking of "coming *in His glory*"?

A. (See verse 31.)

Q. To what does Jesus compare Himself in this parable?

A. To a king on a throne (verses 31, 34), assigning to his subjects such rewards as they deserve. (Rom. xiv. 10.)

Q. What are all the good compared to, in verse 32?

A. To sheep.

Q. What are all the bad compared to?

A. To goats. (Ezek. xxxiv. 17–24.)

Q. Why are the good said to be placed on the right hand of the Saviour in His kingdom, and the bad on the left (verse 33)?

A. In the Jewish courts, on the right hand of the judge was a place of honor; but on the left a place of disgrace.

Q. By whom is Christ appointed thus to exercise judgment?

A. (See St. John v. 22.)

Q. In what touching words does Jesus address those who have been faithful?

A. He calls them "ye blessed of my Father."

Q. What does He invite them to come and enjoy?

A. The peace and purity and all the happy employments of the heavenly life, which were prepared and intended for them from the beginning of things (verse 34).

Q. What actions are mentioned as having been performed by these faithful persons?

A. (Verses 35, 36.)

Q. But as Jesus is not among us in a mortal form, how can *we* perform similar good actions, and gain His approbation?

A. (Verse 40.)

Q. What, then, should we do now?

A. We should look around to find those who need our sympathy and assistance, and feed the hungry, be kind to strangers, clothe the destitute, visit the sick, and pity the prisoner. (St. James i. 27.)

Q. If we do this with true zeal for Christ, how will it be regarded?

A. We shall be blessed for it, as if it were a service rendered directly to Jesus on earth.

Q. What is the import of verses 37 and 38?

A. These real friends of the Saviour are represented as disclaiming any merit, and as being surprised that their good deeds should be mentioned.

Q. What do we call this feeling?

A. Humility, or an humble opinion of one's own character and deserts.

Q. Must not every real Christian feel that after all he is very deficient, and has done far less than he ought to do, when he remembers what God and his Saviour have done for him?

A. His humility will increase as his Christian life grows.

Q. How is it made plain that we serve and please our great Master, when we do good to mankind?

A. (See verse 40.)

Q. Whom does the pure and holy Jesus condescend to call His "brethren"?

A. The whole human family; even *we* are the objects of His tender and affectionate regard.

Q. What fearful sentence is pronounced on the wicked, or those on the left hand?

A. (Verse 41.)

Q. What are the wicked then to dread?

A. Banishment from the happy society of the good into the spiritual darkness, where all evil and corrupt spirits dwell in unspeakable misery. (2 Thess. i. 7–10.)

Q. On whom must this punishment fall?

A. (See verses 42, 43.)

Q. How does the contrast between these two classes, the good and the evil, come out yet more clearly in verse 44?

A. The evil are proud, and pretend that they *have* done their duty; while the good, who have really done it, feel ashamed of their shortcomings.

Q. But is there any such thing as deceiving the Great Judge?

A. We can never deceive Him, for He knows all the secrets of our hearts. (Ps. cxxxix. 2.)

Q. What answer, then, must the sinful receive?

A. They must be told that whenever they are unfaithful to any duty, — whenever they are selfish, sensual, passionate, or profane, — they directly offend against the pure spirit of Jesus Christ, as much as if His bodily form were before their eyes at the moment (verse 45).

Q. How is the whole parable concluded?

A. (Verse 46.)

Q. What, then, is the portion of the wicked?

A. Spiritual wretchedness inconceivable.

Q. What is the portion of the righteous?

A. Spiritual joy, life, peace, deeper and higher than we can now fully understand.

Q. When did these judgments, indicated in this parable, begin to be executed?

A. Immediately after the time of Christ, and especially at the destruction of the Jewish nation, when the unrighteous were severely punished.

Q. How long will these judgments continue to go on?

A. As long as we continue to be conscious and responsible beings; that is, forever.

Q. Where, then, is the only way of safety, as well as our highest and most precious privilege?

A. In repenting of our sins, and in receiving the Lord Jesus Christ into our hearts, by faith, to be to us both a Saviour from our sins, and our Eternal Life. (St. John iii. 16; 1 St. John v. 12–15.)

THE END.

www.ingramcontent.com/pod-product-compliance
Lightning Source LLC
Chambersburg PA
CBHW031455160426
43195CB00010BB/982